Life in Full Stride

Life in Full Stride

FAITH-STRETCHING REFLECTIONS
FOR CHRISTIANS IN THE REAL WORLD

Charles R. Ringma

REGENT COLLEGE PUBLISHING
Vancouver, British Columbia

Life in Full Stride
Copyright © 2004 Charles R. Ringma
All rights reserved.

This edition published 2004 by Regent College Publishing
in association with Piquant Agency

Regent College Publishing
5800 University Boulevard, Vancouver, BC V6T 2E4 Canada
www.regentpublishing.com

First published (1996) in the Philippines by
OMF Literature Inc.
776 Boni Avenue,
Mandaluyong City, Metro Manila

Views expressed in works published by Regent College Publishing
are those of the authors and do not necessarily represent the official
position of Regent College <www.regent-college.edu>.

Unless otherwise noted, all Scripture quotations are from the
New International Version of the Bible,
copyright © 1973, 1978 by the International Bible Society.
Used by permission of Zondervan Publishers.

National Library of Canada Cataloguing in Publication Data

Ringma, Charles
Life in full stride : faith-stretching reflections for Christians
in the real world / Charles Ringma.

ISBN 1-57383-320-7

1. Christian life. I. Title.

BV4501.3.R55 2004   248.4   C2004-902061-7

CONTENTS

Adventure 13

Faith 27

Courage 43

Prayer 59

Hope 73

Realism 85

Forgiveness 101

Obedience 115

Community 145

Service 163

Justice 181

Celebration 197

Reflection 209

Passion 227

Action 243

AMEN 261

To Rock Manuel,
outstanding graduate of the Asian Theological Seminary,
Metro Manila, church planter among the urban poor,
man of vision, but above all, man of God.

PREFACE

These reflections come out of real life experiences. With a great deal of thankfulness, I acknowledge the value I have gained from such diverse experiences as working with aboriginal people in Western Australia, time as a compositor in the printing industry, work as a senior research assistant at a university, years as a high school teacher, many years of theological training, work in several parishes, a long stint of ministry with drug-dependent and troubled young people, and a period of training leaders in Asia. From the people I met, and the diversity of these circumstances, I have learned much.

Equally significant has been the warm and caring family life that my wife Rita has provided together with our four children, Marina, Renay, Leighton and Jodie. Also important has been the friendship that I enjoyed with members of Jubilee Fellowship in Brisbane, with co-workers at Teen Challenge and colleagues at the Department of Social Work and Social Policy of the University of Queensland, and at the Asian Theological Seminary in Metro Manila.

My special thanks to Annette Ganter and Karen McColm for typing these meditations from handwritten notes. My further thanks to Renay and Carsten Larsen for preparing this manuscript for publication and to Letty Paler and other editors at OMF LIT for doing the editorial work.

Brisbane and Metro Manila, 1996

INTRODUCTION

These meditations are a reflection on life in the light of Scripture. They deal with many of the issues of daily living examining these in the mirror of the Bible. They are, I trust, an encouragement to live life realistically and in hope.

Spirituality cannot be an escape from reality. Instead, it is an approach to life nurtured by the belief that God in Christ enters our situation to empower us to live according to his will and purpose. We are, therefore, encouraged to take life seriously in all its personal, family, social, economic, cultural and political dimensions. Christianity does not simply prepare us for heaven but empowers us to live here in ways that glorify God, enhance the well-being of others, and transform our world.

At the same time, Christianity also offers a powerful hope. It reminds us that God's kingdom and the power of his Spirit are among us; things can change, and that a better world is possible. It further reminds us that the grace of God can affect human destiny, that God can act into the world in ways beyond our willing and doing, and that he has the final word.

These meditations, therefore, call us away from a super-spiritual form of Christianity which stresses the spiritual but neglects the natural, and which longs for the heavenly but does not face the earthly. It suggests that such a form of Christianity is an escapism unbecoming of believers whom God has placed as responsible agents on this earth. Instead, these meditations call us to a realism characterized by hope, a faith marked by prayer, a realism that faces life in all its challenges and difficulties, and which seeks to be responsible.

But being responsible does not mean that we simply grit our teeth and go it alone. This has frequently led people to cynicism and despair. Rather, responsibility should involve us in partnership—a partnership with God and his people as we seek to respond to the challenges of life.

It is my hope that these reflections will move us from a *world-denying* to a *world-affirming* spirituality. It is my prayer that we let our spirituality be practical and our praxis marked with prayer and faith so that God may take the little that is in our hands and make it much for his glory.

ADVENTURE

REFLECTION 1

THE SPIRIT OF ADVENTURE:

The call to move forward

So do not fear, for I am with you; do not be dismayed, for I am your God. I will strengthen you and help you; I will uphold you with my righteous right hand.

Isaiah 41:10

We are not to be afraid of life, and we are not to be overly careful and calculating. If we wish to move forward, we must take risks. Christ's call to freedom involves taking risks. He invites us to reach out and grasp the new.

This does not mean that we should wildly dive into any and every project. We do need to be discerning, to wait and pray. Yet we will never have ironclad certainty about anything, not even as a result of our carefully devised plans or faithful prayers. Sometimes, we just have to move forward. Living by faith and obedience is not without its challenges.

The Holy Spirit calls us forward. Agnes Sanford describes adventure in this way: "I would not go all of my life in the bondage of heading only on a known path lest I step upon a snake. I would go through the untrodden country toward the goal of my choice, whether or not I trod upon a snake."

This approach to life is not wild and reckless. It is an expression of the impulse to be free. It is born of the desire to express our faith. Such an outlook on life helps us to attempt to realize our goals. This sense of adventure gives life a particular quality. It also puts us on the road to true achievement.

For some, the challenge is not to embark on the road of adventure for the *first time*, but to step out again after failure. This involves overcoming the pain of disappointment and despair, and trying again. Scripture is full of the exhortation: do not be afraid, try again. This requires courage. But this will certainly plunge us into the adventure of life once more.

Prayer: Father, grant that I may never stop dreaming, planning and hoping. Grant that fear or past disappointments may not hold me back from embarking on new dreams and plans. AMEN.

REFLECTION 2

IN THE WORLD AND NOT AFRAID:

Living for the kingdom

The field is the world, and the good seed stands for the sons of the kingdom. The weeds are the sons of the evil one.
                                                    Matthew 13:38

Jesus was not an ascetic. He did not withdraw from life in order to be holy. He socialized, partied, relaxed with friends. He "was about his Father's business." Often he was about that business in his socializing. Jesus' life was not divided between spiritual issues and secular affairs. His life was holistic and integrated.

As Jesus' followers, our lives should also be holistic and integrated. We should not be characterized by defensiveness or fear. Christianity is not a flight from reality. It is precisely the opposite. Christianity is embracing and impregnating reality with the love of God. As Christians, we do not need to be fearful or defensive; we do not need to hide or be apologetic. We should not be embarrassed to try to follow the words and life of Jesus. Many have followed Gandhi, and even Hitler had his supporters. How much more should we show our allegiance to Jesus!

If Jesus could live joyfully and purposefully, so can we as we are sustained by his Spirit. We are sown as good seed in the world. There we live, love, work and strive. There we build our families and businesses. There we experience joy and friendship as well as suffering and pain.

In this, we are no different from other people except that we draw our hope from Jesus whom we worship as Lord, and we work to establish God's kingdom of justice and mercy in this world.

Jesus was no Utopian dreamer envisaging a world for Christians only. He knew that both the good and the bad would remain until the end of the age. Yet he appeared not to be concerned about what the sons of the Evil One could do to us. He told us to live confidently in the midst of a fallen world.

The focus of Jesus is so radically different from ours. Our insecurities and fears cause us to spend too much time reacting negatively to the world. We become known for our criticisms rather than our actions. Jesus suggests that we should get on with living for the kingdom and work out our positive plans and programs. We need to develop a far greater confidence in what it means to be sons and daughters of God and to live that out in the world.

Prayer: Lord, may my life in this world be characterized not by arrogance nor by fear nor by defensiveness, but may I live purposively in doing that which pleases you. AMEN.

REFLECTION 3

THERE ARE SURPRISES:
Celebrating God's generosity

Instead of bronze I will bring you gold, and silver in place of iron. Instead of wood I will bring you bronze, and iron in place of stone.
Isaiah 60:17a

The Christian life is much more than simply a matter of just returns. It is not a matter of giving so much to God so that he will give something back to us. God is not a divine Accountant. We cannot bribe him with the line "because I have been good, I expect you to bless me in some special way."

Sadly, this manner of thinking and operating has become the way we so often relate not only to God but also to other people. So we tend to visit only those who visit us, give to those who are generous to us, and love those who love us. Much of our response thus becomes performance-based and reciprocal in nature.

This can even seep its way into the relationships we have with our spouse and children. Children thus grow up with the idea that they are only loved if they are good; wives gain the impression that they are only appreciated if they perform well at home or in the bedroom.

My point is not however that we can expect God or others to treat us well if we respond shabbily and irresponsibly. The point is that God's attitude to us is characterized by grace and generosity, not by a book-keeper's mentality. Indeed, if that were the case, we all would be on the wrong side of the ledger.

God, in fact, surprises us. He gives when we least expect it; forgives when we do not deserve it; He is patient when time has really run out. His graciousness changes the quality of our lives.

Having been treated like this by God, we cannot but do the same to others. Do the extra for your most difficult and unresponsive child! At Christmas time, give to those who cannot possibly give back to you! Invite to your home those who may have little to give in return! Let us love even when we have been hurt, give when we have not received, and forgive even when forgiveness has not been sought. If God can surprise us, we can try to do the same for others.

Prayer: Lord, thank you so much that your generosity far exceeds my expectations and deserving. Thank you that you do surprise me when I least expect it and give to me even when I have not asked. AMEN.

REFLECTION 4

DON'T PITCH YOUR TENT:

Discipleship is a journey

Rabbi, it is good for us to be here. Let us put up three shelters one for you, one for Moses and one for Elijah.

Mark 9:5

Discipleship involves a journey; it is not simply a spiritual experience. Discipleship is responding to Jesus' call throughout our whole life. From the vigour and enthusiasm of youth to the maturity of old age, the disciple of Jesus makes obedience to the Master's call the central priority.

This means that every spiritual experience is only a step on the road of commitment; it is not where the road ends. This is so no matter how great our experience may have been.

The thrill of conversion, power from an infilling of the Holy Spirit, the rapture of a vision, the impact of a prophecy and the return of wholeness through healing can all constitute significant spiritual experiences for us. So can the experience of solitude, the joy of contemplation and the power of the eucharist.

All of these and other spiritual experiences are not terminal points however. They are not holy ground where we build a shrine. They are certainly not the bases on which we can claim that we have arrived.

Every spiritual experience is simply food for the journey. It is hope for the struggle; fire for the cold winds of disappointment; power for the fight. It is never an end in itself.

The disciples wanted to pitch a tent at the transfiguration of Jesus. They were happy to call a halt at this amazing phenomenon. After all, what more could they ask?

It is appropriate to long for the mountain of transfiguration where our vision is renewed and our hope rekindled. However, such mountains need to be descended; we need to go back to the world; we must share with others the healing power and love of Jesus (Mark 9:14-29).

Prayer: Lord, thank you for every experience and blessing you have given me. Help me not to be satisfied with what I have of you, but grant me the grace to press on to love you more and serve you more faithfully. AMEN.

REFLECTION 5

DO NOT FORGET TO DANCE:

Celebrating in the midst of life

Be sure to set aside a tenth of all that your fields produce each year. Eat the tithe of your grain, new wine and oil, and the firstborn of your herds and flocks in the presence of the Lord your God.
Deuteronomy 14:22-23

We can very easily become burdened with the tasks at hand. Demanding children, endless housework, stressful jobs, educational concerns and a difficult ministry. Difficulties are often compounded by relationship problems and nearly always by the pressures we place on ourselves to do things well, or better, or to be the best.

In all of this we can easily begin to feel overwhelmed. Life becomes a burden; happiness goes out the window.

Some respond to these circumstances by wistfully planning the next holiday where they hope to recoup their energies. A more permanent solution, however, is to plan regular personal space for quietude and renewal in the midst of our busy lives. As part of that renewal we need to learn how to celebrate.

One need not be rich in order to learn the art of celebration. Negro slaves in a white oppressive America knew how to sing, tell stories, laugh and celebrate far more than their rich masters. In fact, "having little" rather than "having much" can be the seedbed for celebration as it is born out of creative simplicity.

Coffee, tea or snacks with friends. Breakfast in the park. A special meal. Reminiscing with friends. A night of celebration where a friend is honoured. A party for no reason at all except to celebrate. A late afternoon walk. Reading poetry. Listening to music. A special night of love-making. An evening of story-reading with the family or special games at home. The list could go on.

We all have our own ideas about relaxation, and celebration takes different forms for different people. But, in the midst of life, let us not forget to dance. If the Israelites were allowed to party on their tithes and offerings to the Lord, then surely we can celebrate with a portion from the labour of our hands.

Prayer: Lord, thank you that gaiety, fun, laughter and celebration are to be part of the life you have given us. AMEN.

REFLECTION 6

THE MEEK ARE NOT WEAK:

The appropriate use of power

Blessed are the meek, for they shall inherit the earth.
                                                    Matthew 5:5

Christians are sometimes portrayed as being weak, gullible, wimpish and self-effacing. The German philosopher Nietzsche claimed that Jesus also was weak. He claimed that Christians and their Christ lacked the will to power.

Power is precisely what the issue is all about! But the question is: What form of power does God want us to exercise? Is it a power that overwhelms and controls the other, or power that sets limitations on ourselves and seeks to serve and free the other? Clearly it is the latter. The significant exercise of power over our own selves is called meekness.

Moses was called the meekest man in all the earth (Numbers 12:3). He was not weak. In fact, he was a great leader in Israel's history. Yet Moses' power was never for self-aggrandizement. His power lay in his concern for the welfare of God's people and in his persistence to seek God's direction for the nation. His power lay in his ability to hear from God and execute his plans.

Jesus later called himself "meek and lowly in heart" (Matthew 11:29 KJV). He was hardly a weak personality. He demonstrated an ability to shape his own destiny and that of his followers in spite of great opposition and eventual death. Jesus was never intimidated, but with singleness of heart, he lived out his Father's will and purpose.

We are called to express power through meekness. In the original Greek, meekness means controlled strength. It is used to describe a horse that has been broken in to the use of bit and bridle, and thus prepared for useful service. The meek are those who have learned the virtue of self-control. They have embraced the call to live under God's discipline and in the way of his wisdom.

The meek are not weak. They have enthusiasm for life and its challenges. They have a sense of adventure, but they draw on God for inspiration, direction and empowerment. They have power over themselves so they can serve others better.

Prayer: Lord, help me to be tough on myself so that I can be gentle with others. AMEN.

FAITH

REFLECTION 7

THE FAITH OF THE FAITHFUL:

Trusting God when the going gets tough

Women received back their dead, raised to life again. Others were tortured and refused to be released, so that they might gain a better resurrection.

Hebrews 11:35

We all like to succeed. We would all like to win mighty victories. We would have no difficulty signing up for the exhilarating drama at Jericho when the walls fell "after the people had marched around them for seven days" (Hebrews 11:30). But we would be more than happy to opt out rather than be in solidarity with believers who "went about in sheepskins and goatskins, destitute, persecuted and mistreated" (11:37b). These people not only experienced failure, but they were forced to hide in "caves and holes in the ground" to save their own skins (11:38b).

It is, therefore, all the more surprising that these failures were commended for their faith (11:39a). Clearly then, faith has little to do with success and everything with faithfulness. This suggests that faith with signs may be of a lesser quality than faith without them. It is one thing to trust God and receive the desired outcome. It is another to trust God when nothing has changed.

It seems that most of us have lived through both experiences. Answers and silences, victories and apparent defeats are our common lot. These can leave us a bit puzzled. Sometimes we can even become angry, if not embittered. Resolving these struggles in faith, so that we can still go on trusting and loving, is every time a great victory.

Prayer: Lord, grant that my faith may be centred in who you are, rather than in the blessings you may choose to give. AMEN.

REFLECTION 8

THE PRAYER OF FAITH:

"Carrying" the one in need

Some men came, bringing to him a paralytic, carried by four of them.
Mark 2:3

Sometimes people are so distraught and burdened that all faith and hope have ebbed out of their lives. In my experience many such people readily come to mind: drug addicts, prostitutes, and those who have made unsuccessful attempts on their own lives.

But the well-to-do and outwardly successful can also be inwardly distraught and in deep despair. The only difference between these two groups is not their sense of need but their willingness to acknowledge it. The former group is usually much more open than the latter. After all, if you are successful, you are supposed to "have it all together."

Both groups of people equally need help. Our preparedness to "carry" them for a period of time until their own faith and hope are restored can be a vital life-link. This is precisely what the prayer of faith is all about. It is the willingness to spiritually "carry" people for a time until hope is renewed. It is the preparedness to pray for them, to believe for their well-being and growth, and to envisage them whole and strong.

The prayer of faith also has a practical dimension. It involves providing help, support and encouragement. The four helpers of the paralytic exercised precisely such a role. They believed for the paralytic that Jesus could help. They assumed the practical responsibility to get him to Jesus. And they were not easily put off even though a big crowd was in the way. They pressed on in faith and brought their friend to the Master.

There are times when we need to play that role for others. When life has dealt a cruel blow, when there has been rejection, when wrong moral choices have had an undermining effect, and hope is gone, then we need to pray and work on their behalf in such a way that new life will come. And when it does, our task is done. We then need to step aside and allow the other to get on with his or her own life.

Prayer: *Lord, make me an instrument of your healing.* AMEN.

REFLECTION 9

WHEN GOD IS SILENT:

Faithfulness in the face of absence

The secret things belong to the Lord our God, but the things revealed belong to us and to our children forever, that we may follow all the words of this law.

Deuteronomy 29:29

God has spoken and acted in history. Some of this activity has been recorded in Scripture. In our day, God continues to act and speak. Much of this action is the work of God's Spirit in the church, although God also works sovereignly in human history.

But there are also times when God appears to be silent. This occurs particularly when we have reduced God's action to predictable routines, and go about our religious duties without any sense of joy, direction or enthusiasm. It can also occur when we experience burnout or when we walk the mysterious path of the dark night of the soul. At these times God's silence can become particularly acute: we do not sense his presence with us, our prayers do not appear to be heard or answered; there appears to be little direction in our lives, so we easily feel lost. Moreover, we can become weighed down by guilt and frustration.

It appears that these experiences are not uncommon. The psalmist cries out, "O God, do not keep silent; be not quiet, O God, be not still" (Psalm 83:1). And again, "But I cry to you for help, O LORD; in the morning my prayer comes before you. Why, O LORD, do you reject me and hide your face from me?" (Psalm 88:13,14).

The psalms are full of such complaints, and while there aren't any easy answers, several important things stand out. First, God is big enough to be able to cope with our complaints. Secondly, we can be thankful and hopeful on the basis of what God has done for us in the past. Thirdly, we need to acknowledge the problems *we* have with waiting. Fourthly, we need to get on with doing what we have already been given to do. And finally, we can test the depth of our commitment by being faithful when the support structures appear to have vanished, and God has become silent. Loyalty should operate not only when God is present, active and giving, but also when God appears to be absent.

Prayer: Lord, I am amazed at how easily I get shaken when things do not go the way I expect or desire. Help me to be faithful even when you feel so far away. AMEN.

REFLECTION 10

PLANT THOSE FRUIT TREES:

Doing what we must

It will be good for those servants whose master finds them ready, even if he comes in the second or third watch of the night.

Luke 12:38

I have met Christians who continually put their lives on hold. They have stopped making important decisions and fail to get on with the business of life. Some were influenced by the idea that Jesus would soon come back, and therefore there was little point in making long-term decisions.

Others I have met were waiting for some special word from God to be fulfilled. This had to do with some important ministry they believed they were to embark on. As a consequence, decisions regarding housing, schooling, work and family matters were all suspended. For some this dragged on for several years. And when their plans for ministry did not push through, their family suffered even more.

Others have put their lives on hold due to serious illness with only a limited time to live.

But the majority I have met are those who are always waiting for something special to happen: waiting to accumulate a lot of money, to get a promotion, to find the right life partner, or to be recognized in ministry. The problem with this approach to life is that it does not recognize that we are called to get on with living in the present, with faithfulness and integrity.

This is not to deny that there may be important future events for which we need to prepare. But it does reject the idea that we are to sit around and not go about our basic responsibilities while waiting for our dreams to come true.

God wants us to be faithful in doing the tasks of the present. Martin Luther once commented that he would still plant his apple trees on Tuesday if he knew that the Lord was coming back on Wednesday.

Prayer: Lord, help me to be faithful in the things at hand, even while I wait in faith for you to prepare me for the things that lie ahead. AMEN.

REFLECTION 11

IF YOU HAVE DONE IT BEFORE:
Remaining dependent on God's enabling

I asked your disciples to drive out the spirit, but they could not.
Mark 9:18b

The first time we performed some Christian activity we probably put in a lot of prayer and preparation. Just go back to the first time you led a Bible study, a prayer meeting or preached a sermon. Or try to remember the prayer and planning you put into the youth club you started, or the Christian organization you got under way. What about the first time you sang solo in church, or prophesied? Inexperience, apprehension, even fear can drive us to prayer asking God to help us successfully execute our tasks.

With time, inexperience can turn to confidence. We can eventually become so competent that we can perform tasks without much preparation and sometimes even without much prayer. The problem in this does not lie in our increasing expertise in a particular area. We should never belittle the value of competence, for this can help us to work more efficiently and effectively. The problem, however, is that we readily fall into the trap of self-sufficiency. We rely too much on our expertise. We perform our tasks just as well without prayer—or so it seems.

But, in fact, we cannot. Thinking that we can shows that a subtle, but very significant shift has taken place. That shift reflects not only our smugness but also our failure to remember that situations vary and, in fact, each one is unique. No two congregations nor two counsellees are ever the same. Each situation requires its own particular sensitivity and its own peculiar blessing. Hence the prayer for wisdom, discernment, sensitivity, flexibility and love is always needed and appropriate.

The disciples of Jesus failed in their attempt to help the boy in distress. It was not their first time to deal with demon possession (Mark 6:13). But they had become self-reliant. Jesus, therefore, rebukes them for their lack of faith and prayer. Expertise clearly undermined their effectiveness, and their previous experience prevented them from being flexible. No amount of experience, however, should lessen our need to seek God's wisdom and power for each situation.

Prayer: Lord, help me always to be open to your help and your work in and through me in each situation. AMEN.

REFLECTION 12

THE BASIS OF OUR SECURITY:

Trust in God

And without faith it is impossible to please God, because anyone who comes to him must believe he exists and that he rewards those who earnestly seek him.

Hebrews 11:6

Ours is a troubled world. Our inner world can be equally troubled as we search for security.

There is much that can shake our inner certainty. We do not always realize our dreams and ambitions. And plans and projects do not always work out the way we had hoped.

Moreover, we are often mixed in our motives for seeking to do good and are downright devious in doing wrong. All these mean that for many of us, a battle continues to smoulder or rage in our innermost being.

Finding a central core of security with which we can undergird this battle becomes a pressing issue.

One oft-tried remedy is to seek security in our previous spiritual experiences. But these tend not to provide long-term security. This is not because these experiences have not been genuine, but experiences are fleeting and impermanent. Thus we cannot find the central core of certainty in past spiritual experiences.

God himself must be the central core of our certainty. However, our relationship with God is always reciprocal: He calls us and we respond in faith. Our central core of security is as weak or as strong as the faith we continue to exercise (with God's help) in his providential care, and in the trustworthy nature of his word and promises.

Thus security in God is always relational. It is based on God's faithfulness and *our trust* in him. God is the eternal "I am that I am." He does not change in his love towards us. But our security can only lie in our trust in him who is faithful in his commitment towards us.

Prayer: Lord, help me not to place my quest for certainty and security in anything other than you. Help me to let go of particular spiritual experiences, plans and projects which have been so very important to me. Help me instead to continue to look to you to sustain me and to give me new life. AMEN.

REFLECTION 13

A SUNDAY SCHOOL FAITH IN AN ADULT WORLD:

Developing a mature faith

Then we will no longer be infants, tossed back and forth by the waves, and blown here and there by every wind of teaching.

Ephesians 4:14a

In Sunday School we learned that God is big, powerful and good, that he helps those who are kind and is against those who are bad. In the world of the young everything is right or wrong. The good triumphs and evil is over-thrown.

In the adult world, our Sunday School faith can often be shaken. There, good and bad are not always so easily definable. The good doesn't always triumph. God does not always seem to act on behalf of those who love him. In fact, life appears to be contradictory. We are often stuck for answers, particularly in the face of evil and tragedy. We find life to be complex and our faith often appears to be inadequate.

Sadly, some find that their faith has been made totally inadequate by the reality of the adult world and they jettison their faith. Others remain spiritually faithful, but struggle trying to find faith's relevance and applicability to life.

In the process of survival we need to move beyond our Sunday School faith. Just as we can not graft an oak or a mango tree onto a sunflower, we certainly cannot expect our adult experience to be sustained by a Sunday School faith. Such a faith needs to grow up.

Adult faith understands that God has revealed himself not only in power but also in weakness. It sees that while some of God's action is in the present, much of it is also future. It understands that suffering is as much a part of our life as the victory that God gives us. Moreover, it knows that evil is still a part of this world even though Christ has died to eradicate it.

The challenge is for our faith to grow up. It needs to be intellectually nurtured and spiritually stimulated. It needs to face life's questions with a boldness that knows what it believes and why it believes. Maturing faith involves not only a growing attitude of heart but also a continuing sharpening of the mind in order to understand God's Word for our lives and times.

Prayer: Lord, may my faith in you become more honest, open and strong. Help me to face all the questions of life with faith and trust in you. AMEN.

COURAGE

REFLECTION 14

COURAGE TO GO ON:

Embracing a new calling

That I may boast on the day of Christ that I did not run or labour for nothing.

Philippians 2:16

It is seldom the heat of the moment or the immediate pressure of the task that causes us to falter. It is our feeling of being undermined or our being disillusioned that makes the task difficult. Thus it is not so much the difficulties that cause us to falter but gnawing uncertainty, when we begin to doubt and to question the rightness or purpose of what we are doing.

James Michener, in his novel *The Covenant*, tells of a remarkable Bantu custom. When lack of rain and green pastures forced Bantus to move great distances to find new watering spots and hunting terrain, the women joyfully carried large eggs containing their essential water supply. While the eggs were full and heavy the women walked with light step. But as the days dragged on and their physical burden became lighter, their hearts became heavier and their gait slower. For with the lightness of their physical burden, their hope of survival slowly ebbed away.

Similarly, we can have light hearts even though the burden is great. We can also have heavy hearts even when our burdens are light. This has everything to do with our sense of purpose. If our life goals are clear to us, we can continue even in the face of great difficulty. If we begin to doubt the wisdom of what we are doing, strength begins to falter.

It is at such a time that each of us needs to ask the hard questions: Why did I begin in the first place? What motivated me? Did God really call me? Am I doing this because it is right or simply because I want to be successful? Is it time for me to stand aside, for others can do it better? Is God calling me to something else? These questions can be endless and the process difficult, but face these we must. There is little point in continuing when the heart for it and the sense of calling are gone. More particularly, we should not continue when it is clearly time to do something else.

Tasks done sparingly or grudgingly for God are not worth doing. Kingdom service deserves more than the scraps of our enthusiasm. If we deem it right to continue, we need to find new energy for the present task and a rekindled hope for the future. Knowing that it is right for us to do what we are doing refuels us. And if we need to pursue another objective, the vision itself will empower us.

Prayer: Lord, help me to re-evaluate what I am doing. Give me the grace to go on as you re-confirm your will for me. But help me also to change direction when the time for that has come. AMEN.

REFLECTION 15

AS SMALL AS A MUSTARD SEED:
Taking hold of small dreams

The kingdom of heaven is like a mustard seed, which a man took and planted in his field. Though it is the smallest of all your seeds, yet when it grows, it is the largest of garden plants and becomes a tree, so that the birds of the air come and perch in its branches.
Matthew 13:31-32

Dreams usually do not come to us in completed form. They come as starting points. On these we need to build. Thus an idea comes and we ponder on it, work on it and finally begin to see some results. From small hopes, ideas, insights, inspirations, inner nudges and dreams, great plans and actions may evolve.

It is true that while some of our dreams grow into reality, many of our thoughts, ideas, wishes and initial plans simply evaporate. They have come to nothing. Some would say that these were never meant to be, otherwise they would have come to fruition. But this may be far too easy an explanation. It is deterministic, with the rationalization that whatever will be, will be.

We need to see ourselves as creators and see life as open with its possibilities and potential. Therefore, we need to take hold of our thoughts and dreams. We need to plant them carefully. They need to be nurtured with prayer so that they may grow into things useful and purposeful. This is what creating is all about. It is believing that not everything that we think or dream about is impossible.

Some thoughts and dreams may be God's direction for our lives. The Holy Spirit will give discernment. But we must be prepared to make some commitment—be prepared to run the risk of putting time, energy and resources into those thoughts in order to bring them to fruition. This requires courage as well as faith.

Sadly, we often throw our best seeds away. We too quickly dismiss something as being impossible: "I could never do that." Or we say, "God would not entrust me with something like that." But good seed, even though a small mustard seed, needs to be recognized for its potential and planted in good soil.

Prayer: Lord, help me to grasp new thoughts with all their possibilities, because I believe that you are working creatively within me and guiding my life. AMEN.

REFLECTION 16

BROKEN FRIENDSHIPS:

Learning to love again

Even my close friend, whom I trusted, he who shared my bread, has lifted up his heel against me.

Psalm 41:9

Not too many of us go through life with all our friendships and relationships intact. People pass through our lives and go elsewhere and we subsequently lose contact. The cessation of friendship need not of itself be a painful experience. But when friendships are ruptured due to misunderstanding, intrigue and unfaithfulness, we can be deeply wounded. The deeper the friendship and the greater the trust, the greater the pain and disappointment.

Some people resolve never *fully* to love and trust others again after such an experience. They draw a cloak about themselves and withdraw. Others are pained to the point of cynicism. But we need to grieve our way through broken friendships so we can live with renewed vitality.

No matter how much we may try to restore certain broken relationships, some appear to be irredeemable. Too much damage has been done. All we can do then is to acknowledge our part, our failings and our sins in the breakdown. We can thank God for all that was good and beautiful in the former relationship and grieve our own failings. Having made our confession, we can then release the other person to God and forgive the other for hurts inflicted upon us.

In doing this we face the fact that we live in a marred world—a world where the beautiful, the good and the true become caricatures and turn out to be the opposite of what we had hoped and desired.

Jesus must surely have felt the same. Even to the very last, Jesus offered his friendship to Judas only to have it rejected (John 13: 26, 27). Yet life had to go on for Jesus even at this critical point, and so it must for us. When we grieve over broken friendships and forgive, we can love again.

Prayer: Lord, give me the grace to grieve over that which I cannot redeem and help me to learn to love and trust again. AMEN.

REFLECTION 17

CERTAINTY TO ACT:

Being bold in obedience

The LORD had said to Abram, "Leave your country, your people and your father's household and go to the land I will show you"
                                                            Genesis 12:1

God is not there as a cover for our insecurities. He does not want us to be afraid of life and we cannot use him to fight life's battles for us. God is not meant to be a crutch.

To believe in God does not mean that we do not believe in our own abilities. To look to God for help does not mean that we are helpless. It means, rather, that we want to pattern our lives according to God's ways and to please him in the things we do.

We are also to be responsible for ourselves. We are not to be non-persons so that God can be all in all. Instead, we are to be persons of courage, strength and commitment. For this reason (and not just because of our weaknesses) we yield ourselves to God.

When Jesus taught that a man should love God with all his heart and with all his soul and with all his mind (Matthew 22:37), he envisaged a person dynamic in his emotional, volitional and intellectual life, responding to God in love.

In the story of Abram's call to leave his country, we see a vivid picture of this strength of response. Abram, in responding to God's challenge, displayed a certainty that he had heard aright, even though it seemed preposterous that he should pack his bags and leave his country. He was not racked by self-doubt. Abram believed God's word and believed enough in himself to act upon that word. There was no vacillation or irresolution in Abram. There was the willingness to listen. The strength to believe. The courage to obey—to embark on an uncertain journey.

The life of faith is not something that breeds dependence, but, rather, boldness and fortitude. God's word to us always brings the challenge of obedience. That obedience is asked of us as free individuals. In making an obedient response, we affirm our persons as much as we honour God.

Prayer: Lord, thank you that your challenge to obedience does not generate dependence, but maturity and boldness. AMEN.

REFLECTION 18

WHEN GOD CALLS:

Responding to the nudges of God's Spirit

But Jesus told him, "Follow me, and let the dead bury their own dead."

Matthew 8:22

There is no such thing as an ideal time to serve God. God's call to service often comes at an odd hour. The inner nudge to see or ring someone may come when one has just settled down to relax. The call to the ministry may come at the peak of one's secular career. The challenge to go overseas may come when one is doing particularly well in one's own country.

God's sense of timing and ours do not always match. Some think that the ideal time to serve God is while they are still single. Others claim the opportunity for service comes when the children have grown up.

Clearly, there is no ideal time, but we need to respond when God whispers to us and opportunity knocks. For with God's call comes an energizing and empowering as well. Inconvenience may stare us in the face, but hope rises in our hearts when the Spirit challenges us to take on a particular project.

While the timing may not be to our liking, God's call usually finds us at a point where the old is no longer satisfying and we have begun to look for new direction. More importantly, we need to accept that there is nothing more revitalizing than to know and do what God wants of us.

God's call gives a specific purpose to our life and this empowers us. Working without any sense of purpose or direction is debilitating. Working for and together with God is stimulating even though the going may get tough. Paul was excited to be called to be an apostle of Jesus Christ. This defined his whole life. We need to joyfully seek God's direction for our life and grasp with both hands the things he commissions us to do. To delay responding to his call is to deprive ourselves.

Prayer: Lord, thank you that you do wish to speak to me about my life's direction. Help me to seek your will and purpose and then to do it joyfully. AMEN.

REFLECTION 19

BE REAL:

Facing our strengths and limitations

Do not think of yourself more highly than you ought but rather think of yourself with sober judgment, in accordance with the measure of faith God has given you.

Romans 12:3

Being a Christian has everything to do with faith, hope, courage and trust. We believe that God acts into our lives and that he has the final word. The future is always open. Things can change for the better. But this does not mean that we can be wishy-washy and irresponsible and then hope that things will automatically get better in spite of our mistakes and wrongdoing.

Christians are to face life boldly. This signifies that Christians are to be realists rather than idealists. While our faith is centred on God, we need to be realistic about ourselves. We need to face squarely our weaknesses while recognizing our strengths. We need to acknowledge our sins and failures as well as our achievements and victories.

Paul suggests that our sense of realism should be characterized by neither a sense of inferiority nor by superiority. This means that we need to be fully aware of our positive qualities and the gifts that God bestowed on us. But it also means that we are to be aware of our limitations.

This realistic perspective cannot be achieved if we live in isolation from others. It can only come if we are transparent to others and have relationships which encourage response and feedback. In the context of family, church and work, we can discover something of the truth about ourselves.

Being a real person, however, has nothing to do with being negative or pessimistic. Paul reminds us that our realism must always be evaluated in the light of faith. That means that we accept what is currently true of us but, at the same time, believe that further growth and development are always possible.

Prayer: Lord, I do not want to be a pessimist nor an optimist, but a realist. I want to be realistic about myself and trust you for what I may yet grow into. AMEN.

REFLECTION 20

CHRIST IS ALSO AGAINST US:

The ministry of correction

Yet, I hold this against you.
Revelation 2:4

Unlike those in Asia, Africa and Latin America, Christians in North America and Europe appear to be overly consumed with a search for personal meaning. Increasingly they are looking to the Christian faith to meet their identity needs. One consequence of this emphasis is that their Christian lives are becoming more and more inwardly focused. But even more seriously, they tend to see God as the paternal and almost indulgent father who gives whatever they want. This means that God is always for them and backs their concerns.

Thankfully this picture of the Christian life is partially wrong. If this were not the case, we all would be in serious trouble, for we tend to be our own greatest enemies. Our perceived needs, our concerns and our projects often need to be adjusted. These need to be challenged and changed. That is why we need to appreciate the fact that God also challenges us. He is for us in his love and purpose for our lives. He understands our failings and our mistakes, but he also corrects us. This is something we should welcome.

In human relationships we need the honest feedback of others. We also need God to stand over against us—not as a tyrant or some fearful Being, but as Someone who combines love with firmness, and kindness with justice.

Our plans are not automatically God-honouring, and our ideas are not always in consonance with the kingdom of God. Therefore we need initially to hold our plans lightly. In praying we need to seek God's nod of approval as well as his blessing.

This corrective role is the mark of true friendship. Our friends do not always agree with us. Nor should they. They also need to rebuke us. Thus God's role in correcting us is not at loggerheads with his friendship. Hebrews 12 reminds us, ". . . do not make light of the Lord's discipline, and do not lose heart when he rebukes you, because the Lord disciplines those whom he loves, and he punishes everyone he accepts" (vs. 5-6). This process is never pleasant at the time, but "it produces a harvest of righteousness and peace" (v. 11).

Prayer: Lord, thank you that you are that kind of a friend who cares as well as corrects. Help me to seek your guidance regarding my thoughts and plans. AMEN.

PRAYER

REFLECTION 21

PRAYER:

The opening of our hands

Yet not as I will, but as you will.
									Matthew 26:39

Prayer is one of the important spiritual disciplines of the Christian life. Yet all too often prayer is problematic for us, for our routines in prayer are not maintained, and our much asking frequently appears to be left unanswered.

As a solution, we may need to relearn some aspects of the art of praying. An important starting point is learning to listen. Our fretful praying is not lost to God's ear, but it may produce little benefit. Articulating our own anxieties may be helpful psychologically, but we need to move from our own world to enter the world of the Other.

Essentially, prayer is relationship-building, a communion. Karl Barth once said that "in prayer God invites us to live with him." Conversely, in prayer we invite God to enter into our lives and situations. When that happens, we unleash the possibility of change and renewal. When in quiet surrender, we enter God's world and he ours, and we open ourselves to hear what he might say, prayer becomes fruitful. Rather than our circumstances, it is *we* who may then be changed. Rather than a specific solution to a problem, repentance may well up. Rather than the removal of the difficulty, trust may grow. Our initial prayer may be supplanted by prayers that embrace the higher good. Finally, strength may surface for us to face the issues and to act boldly and courageously.

As we enter God's presence and learn to listen, new convictions may grow within us to pursue new courses of action. Courage may be given to face that which we previously thought impossible to deal with.

Prayer thus becomes that mysterious linking of ourselves with God and he with us. It is not the mere presentation of a request list. Rather, it is the recognition that we do not know what is best for ourselves and others. It is the opening of our hands and hearts to the God who not only speaks but who involves himself in our personal world. In such a communion we will not only have our prayers answered, but we will also be transformed.

Prayer: Lord, I spend far too much time telling you what I think you should do. Help me in prayer to open my heart to you that I might hear what you have to say. AMEN.

REFLECTION 22

AN OPEN EAR:

The art of listening

He wakens me morning by morning, wakens my ear to listen like one being taught. The Sovereign LORD *has opened my ears*
Isaiah 50:4b-5a

Being a Christian has everything to do with listening to God's voice. We often think that the first task of the Christian is action—doing deeds of love and service. But action is to be preceded by obedience, and obedience should flow from listening.

Listening to God is not easy. We find it hard to be still, since so many voices clamour for our attention. These other voices also need to be listened to for they speak to us about family, work or worldly matters. These things cannot be ignored. But if we are going to live a life of quality, we need to get God's perspective on these matters.

God speaks to us in many ways. We have learned that God speaks to us through the Bible, our conscience and our circumstances. But the ways in which God can speak to us are broader than these three. He uses other people to encourage and challenge us. He also speaks to us in dreams and visions. The important thing is not the way God speaks but our ability to be open and receptive.

We are usually more receptive at important transition points in our lives. When a particular phase of our life, or a particular role or task has come to an end, or when we have experienced a crisis or setback, we are usually more open to hear than when life meanders on in its normal course.

Being open at crucial times is what Isaiah is referring to. The Lord was preparing him for suffering and difficulty (Isaiah 50:6).

Yet it is not only in the critical issues of life that we need to seek God's direction. It is also in petty and insignificant things. We need to heed the nudges of God's Spirit to pray for someone, drop a friend a note, send someone some money, go out of our way to relate to a newcomer, invite someone for a meal, thank or encourage someone. We can begin to develop a whole new sense of adventure where we daily ask God to speak to us regarding things, whether great or small, important or mundane.

Prayer: Father, help me to develop a whole new sensitivity to your nudges and promptings, and help me to translate these into practical action. AMEN.

REFLECTION 23

OUR KNOWLEDGE OF GOD:

Seeking a greater revelation

Great is the L%%ORD%% *and most worthy of praise; his greatness no one can fathom. One generation will commend your works to another; they will tell of your mighty acts.*

Psalm 145:3-4

In reality we know very little about God. We may know a lot about biblical history and the theology of the Bible. We also may know a lot about the church, its life, its service, its sacraments, its history and its great sons and daughters. Because we know about these things, we probably think that we are also very knowledgeable about God. For how else can we know of him, but through his word and his actions in the church and in the world? We cannot know him directly but only in signs of his presence in the world. We see, as it were, the footprints in the sand but not the actual person. We see God's hand in his protection over us as he cares for us and guides us.

Often we see God's involvement only after the event, and we are grateful and humbled by his goodness toward us. Thus we learn to know something of who God is in his actions on our behalf. In all this, however, we have to acknowledge that we actually know him very little. We can thank him for his covenant faithfulness to us, but we need to respect him as the wholly Other. The highest heavens cannot contain him. His thoughts are quite unlike our thoughts. His ways are beyond our comprehension.

And this is as it should be. These truths rightly define our relationship to the Creator of this universe. We know something of him, yet we search for more. We are touched by his presence, but we pray for a fuller blessing. We can see dimly, but even so long for our eyes to be fully opened. We touch the edges of his ways, yet hope for a fuller understanding. The little that we know of him sets us on the path to seek for a greater revelation of his presence.

Prayer: Lord, help me to continue to be open so that I may learn more of you. AMEN.

REFLECTION 24

SOLITUDE:

The art of being still

Yet the LORD longs to be gracious to you; he rises to show you compassion. For the LORD is a God of justice. Blessed are all who wait for him.
                                                                Isaiah 30:18

We all need times of rest and refreshment. These times are important so that we can renew our energy, enthusiasm and vision for the future.

Yet withdrawal from normal activity to gain renewal is not always possible. Thus, in our busy and distracting schedules, we need to insert time for prayer and reflection, for silence and being still.

In making such a time, we first need to disengage from all that occupies our attention. We need to lay down our many and often conflicting thoughts. The physical act of slowly putting our hands palms down can symbolize this move to be open and free from distracting thoughts. In turning our hands palms up, we indicate our willingness to listen to what the Holy Spirit may whisper to us.

To create moments of stillness and openness is something we may wish to do frequently during our day. Set times and places can certainly help us in this spiritual discipline.

Being still, at peace and open to God, we acknowledge that he is the source of life and wisdom. We express our need to be renewed and refreshed. It is like loosening a taut elastic band. It relaxes our bodies and minds. It frees our spirits. Looking to God, we are encouraged, enlightened and renewed.

Solitude in the midst of life creates inner peace and rest. Henri Nouwen speaks of solitude as "the movement from the restless senses to the restful spirit." It is not a withdrawal from life. Solitude is never simply a matter of technique. It is much more a redefinition of boundaries and priorities. It is a gift for those who make room for it, and it comes to those who, in knowing they have nothing, look to God as their provider.

Prayer: Lord, help me to make those spaces in my life where your light can shine and your voice can be heard. AMEN.

REFLECTION 25

THE HELPER:

The God alongside us

But the Counselor, the Holy Spirit, whom the Father will send in my name, will teach you all things and will remind you of everything I have said to you.

John 14:26

We often feel that we are alone in life with its challenges and struggles. Sometimes we think that no one understands us. At other times, we believe that we have to do things by ourselves, thinking that no one wants to be involved with us. This sense of isolation is a particular problem in our modern way of life. God's purposes for us, however, are vastly different. He is concerned about relationship and wishes to draw us into a companionship with himself. He himself exists as the community of Father, Son and Holy Spirit.

Through the work of his Holy Spirit he wants to enter into all the facets and phases of our lives. Scripture speaks of the Spirit as Counsellor—we tend to think of the Spirit as helping us only in times of grief. But that is far too restrictive. The Paraclete is the One who is called alongside to help and sustain us. We have to learn to constantly call on him and invite his presence. We have to invite this gentle but persuasive Person into our praying, into our loving, into our church and into our work.

The art of being a good parent, a caring partner or a creative worker cannot be without the Spirit's help. Not only does the Spirit give us gifts, he also wishes to cultivate particular qualities in our lives. Equally important, he wishes to give us wisdom and insight. We all know how often we need precisely that. Since the Spirit tends not "to muscle in" on us, we need to learn to invite this gracious Helper to aid us.

Prayer: Holy Spirit, I invite you to be with me in all the events of this day. In the work of caring, relating, planning, producing, thinking and giving, I ask you to empower me. AMEN.

REFLECTION 26

THANKFULNESS:

A way of life

Always giving thanks to God the Father for everything, in the name of our Lord Jesus Christ.

                                                         Ephesians 5:20

We take most of life for granted. It is often only in difficult times or in crises that we do not. It is usually at such times that we truly appreciate that we have been helped or have survived. However, feeling thankful should not well up in us only at those times. It should characterize our whole way of life.

We truly possess only what we are thankful for. What we take for granted is something that we do not really have; it slips through our fingers. The things that we are thankful for are the things we endow with meaning. These things can be great and momentous, or small and seemingly insignificant. We can be thankful not only for the gifts of life and health, friendship and safety but also for kind words, a beautiful sunset or that things went well at work.

Gratitude is thus an acknowledgement that so much of our life is really a gift. These gifts come from God's generous heart through the loving hands of others. Life itself comes from him and so does joy, well-being, safety, meaning and purpose. In being thankful, we not only please God and give others their rightful due, but we weave a more beautiful pattern into the fabric of our life with others.

Thankfulness puts a melody in our hearts and helps us to see the Source and Giver of life. Gratitude helps us to rightly define ourselves and to see ourselves in a proper light. For we do not make it all happen; we are simply recipients of so much from the Father's hand. We are not wholly the makers of our own destiny; we have been given so much by others. When we have the eyes to see, our whole way of life can be marked by thankfulness and thus by a new inner joy.

Prayer: Lord, give me the eyes to see the blessings that you constantly give to me so that my life may be characterized by thankfulness to you for your grace, blessing and mercy. AMEN.

HOPE

REFLECTION 27

HOPE HAS A FUTURE:

Responding to the God who is ahead of us

There is surely a future hope for you, and your hope will not be cut off.
Proverbs 23:18

If we live in hope, we have a future. If hope dies, then the future dies with it. The person who is without hope can only live with the legacy of the past and the circumstances of the present. Even though the past and the present are not necessarily bad, to have no future is sad news indeed. For nothing is envisaged; what we have now is all there is.

The person who lives in hope, however, while not despising the past nor the present, looks to God who is always ahead of us. Christ is the leader who has gone before us. He is the pioneer of our faith. He is there in front of us leading the way for us to follow. He is the leader who has opened up the future, and it is his Spirit who brings that future into our present. Therefore, the biblical writers can say that we *have tasted* of the powers of the age to come (Hebrews 6:5), and *have already* the deposit of the good things that are yet to come (2 Corinthians 5:5).

The German theologian J. Moltmann rightly points out that "the one who is born again is, as it were, ahead of himself; he lives from the thing that is coming to him, not from what is already in him." For the one who lives in hope, there is a future; there is more yet that God will do. There is no closure on any situation, and our own actions and words are never final.

Christian hope is not mere optimism. Optimism believes that things will somehow improve. Our hope is centred in God. It acknowledges that he is ahead of us and he constantly draws us forward into his will and purpose. Hope therefore is as powerful as faith, for with it one believes that it is not we but God who will have the final word.

***Prayer:** Lord, grant that I may not be fatalistic but that I may live in hope that looks to you to act and call me forward.* AMEN.

REFLECTION 28

SILVER AND GOLD HAVE I NONE:
Giving what people need

By faith in the name of Jesus, this man whom you see and know was made strong.

Acts 3:16a

Peter and John had clearly inspired some hope in the cripple lying in the temple gate, hope of receiving some money so that he could continue to eke out a miserable existence of dependency. Yet that was not what they had to offer; they were able to give something far better—not money, but health and new life through Christ's power.

It is all too obvious in our relationships with others that we can not always give them what they hope for or expect. This can make us feel inadequate or even guilty. We would like to be able to meet other people's wishes and needs. But the fact that we can not may in itself be a blessing rather than a handicap, for it provides us with the opportunity to make careful responses.

Firstly, it allows us to look more closely at the needs of the other person rather than, had we the *means*, rushing in and giving assistance or support. In so doing, we often discover that the other person needs something quite different which—surprisingly—we may be able to provide. Secondly, it gently prods us to go to God in prayer. If we have nothing to give when we are confronted with human need, then prayer can begin to provide a way.

All these do not suggest that the giving of material or financial help to a needy person is inappropriate. Practical help can be very important, but it is more important to help the person toward what may be truly needed. That may be new hope, faith, courage, positive self-regard, forgiveness of sins, acceptance, true friendship, peace with God, healing or power to live life more truly and faithfully.

The challenge for us is to *respond*, and not to hide behind excuses.

Prayer: Lord, with your power and grace working in my life, I need not be empty-handed in responding to another's need. AMEN.

REFLECTION 29

GROWTH AND CHOICE:

Realizing my potential

So Lot chose for himself the whole plain of Jordan and set out towards the east. The two men parted company: Abram lived in the land of Canaan, while Lot lived among the cities of the plain and pitched his tents near Sodom. Now the men of Sodom were wicked.

Genesis 13:11,12,13a

We have two things to do in life: one is to develop our *potential*, and the other is to make good *choices*. Both greatly determine the shape of our lives and the extent to which we move from where we are to where we ought to be.

The life that Christ offers us is full of potentiality, but we need to grasp this life with both hands. While we may have the beginnings of life in Christ, we can have it more significantly. While we are in Christ by faith, we can grow more fully in him. While the life of the Spirit has touched and influenced us, he can more radically affect and empower us.

To realize our potential means that we need to be characterized by a holy dissatisfaction, a hunger for more, and an unwillingness to be complacent. We are to be those who continue to ask, seek and knock. We are to be those who struggle and strive to see God's kingly rule become more manifest among us.

It is this desire to move forward, to forge ahead, that should characterize us as Christians. We can not all expect to be the most integrated, balanced, mature, moral, fair, determined, resilient and creative people in the world, even though some Christians are such outstanding people. But we can, in spite of inadequate background, socialization and education, realize our potential in Christ. We can all desire, pray for and search out God's will for our lives as well as for our communities and society.

But realizing our potential is intimately linked to making choices. God does not choose to control us. Instead he treats us as mature sons and daughters. We have the responsibility for making important life choices. We can choose to be mediocre, complacent, inconsistent and selfish. We can choose to be people-pleasing, conforming, and unconcerned about our society.

But we can instead begin to back up our praying for the kingdom of God with practical and costly action. We can choose to serve God more than mammon, to put God's will before our careers, and to pepper our lives with the risks and challenges that come from responding to the gentle nudges of the Spirit.

We all believe that we should be known in the world by something more than our churchgoing and our beliefs. We believe that we should also be marked by a particular quality of life. We would like that quality of life to be one of wholeness, but we know that we are still broken and alienated in so many aspects of our own lives.

What should distinguish us from others, therefore, is not that we have arrived, or have it all together, but rather that we desire to grow in Christ, that we long for his kingdom to be more fully revealed through us, and are prepared to make those choices that seek to obey and serve God in our world. Thus, while we would like to be known for our power, wisdom and wholeness, it is from our weakness, searching, praying and obedience that life will flow.

Prayer: Lord, help me to make life choices that have your kingdom and its values in view. AMEN.

REFLECTION 30

HOPE QUESTIONS OUR CERTAINTIES:

Remaining open to the new

But hope that is seen is no hope at all. Who hopes for what he already has?

Romans 8:24

To have hope means that what we have and are experiencing in the present is not all there is to life. This is tremendously exciting. It means that what we are doing now is not the final act. It also means that what we are doing can bring new possibilities. Hope looks for what is yet to come. It looks to God for his participation and transformation.

To live in hope is so vital for us. For we often think that what we do is so important. We clothe our activities with ultimacy. We think we can control the final outcome of our projects and programs. We tend to deify the past and make absolute our activities.

Hope changes all that. It reminds us that we can not control God's Spirit, for he is like the wind (John 3:8). Hope reminds us that our best and most noble actions are at best partial and imperfect. Moreover, it reminds us that at the end of the day we will not have it all worked out. In fact, we will be in for some ultimate surprises. The "have nots" will receive bountifully. Those who think they have everything will be empty-handed (Matthew 25:37-40).

If in the end things work out rather differently than we expected, this does not mean that there is little purpose in acting meaningfully and decisively in our world. Quite the opposite is true. It simply means that what we do is limited and incomplete and thus requires God's action to take it further, to transform it and to make it fruitful.

In expecting God's participation we can be said to be living in hope. Let us thus acknowledge the limitations of the work of our own hands and celebrate what God is able to do.

Prayer: Lord, when I have done all that I could, I thank you that you can take that further with your blessing and transformation. The small you can make great, and the little you can make much. AMEN.

REFLECTION 31

A SECOND CONVERSION:

Facing the dark night of the soul

But I have prayed for you, Simon, that your faith may not fail. And when you have turned back, strengthen your brothers.

Luke 22:32

When we become Christians, we all wish that life from here on will go fairly smoothly. This clearly is not always the case. Sometimes life becomes even more complicated as we go through the adjustments that being a Christian entails. These adjustments come as a result of God's Spirit fine-tuning us to live in God-honouring ways.

There are also times when God seems so distant that we doubt whether we will ever again experience his presence. This deeply troubling experience sometimes occurs when we are emotionally or physically exhausted in the midst of active ministry. We may be busy praying, preaching and helping others with equally positive results, but there may be a gnawing emptiness in our soul and a sense that God has forsaken us.

The spiritual fathers of the church called this "the dark night of the soul." Here faith no longer enjoys any outward supports. Feelings become numb. The heavens seem like brass. God is seemingly absent and we feel abandoned. At this point we can become overwhelmed by guilt and failure. We burden ourselves with questions that seek an answer for our distress, but we are left with no comfort or solution.

It is in these circumstances that we need to embark on a different course of action. For the more we grope, struggle, analyze ourselves and look for explanations, the more distressed we become. We need, rather, to wait for God to "save" us all over again. This does not mean that we are no longer Christians. It simply means that our Christian life is undergoing a significant transformation.

This heralds a change from a faith with its external supports to a faith that only trusts. From a faith that is secure to one that is uncertain.

There is nothing easy about all this. We do not particularly enjoy the unfamiliar path, but the final outcome is worth the difficulty. For, as a result, our life of faith will be less self-assured and our Christian life less subject to easy explanations and techniques. Moreover, it radically shifts our faith in faith, to faith in God. At the same time, we can be sure that through this difficult time, God is quite capable to "save" us again.

Prayer: Lord, when my certainties are shaken, help me to trust you in the uncertainties. AMEN.

REALISM

REFLECTION 32

A CALL FOR CHRISTIAN HUMILITY:

Being realistic about ourselves

At that time Jesus said, "I praise you, Father, Lord of heaven and earth, because you have hidden these things from the wise and learned, and revealed them to little children."

Matthew 11:25

Christians believe that they are different. They profess that Christ has changed them. They believe that Christ's gift of the Holy Spirit influences them to live a different quality of life. They claim that sinful and negative patterns of living are replaced with a wholesomeness of attitude and behaviour. They rejoice in the fact that they are no longer burdened with unconfessed sins. They believe that Christ has freed them to be their true selves, and that he has given them a new purpose for living and acting in the world. They have changed from living for themselves to living for God and for others.

Moreover, Christians profess that the indwelling Holy Spirit is the *plus* factor in their lives. The Spirit gives them spiritual gifts and abilities such as healing, prophecy and special faith (1 Corinthians 12). The Spirit also gives special wisdom and discernment. Thus Christians can have insight that other people do not have. Moreover, the Spirit empowers and sustains them to serve, help, care and to proclaim the Good News.

All of these should make Christians very special people. One would expect them to stand out amongst their fellows. One would certainly expect that they would be distinctive because of the quality of life they share together in their churches. Joy, care, service, friendship and creativity would be some of the hallmarks of this new life. One would expect that these would flow over into a quality of family life and spill over into the wider areas of social concern. One might expect, therefore, that Christians would be a moral force in the community. That, by demonstrating these qualities, they would trumpet to the wider community what it really means to live.

One would also expect that Christians would stand out in the world of business, in the political sphere and in the institutions of our country. One might even hope that Christians might be the innovators, the trendsetters, the social revolutionaries and the change agents in our community. Yet most of us feel a bit uneasy with this portrayal. This is the ideal. It is what we could be but often are not.

Moreover, our churches often do not reflect this dynamic quality of life. Christian families are also torn by arguments, anger, violence and divorce. Like their neighbours, Christians are also overwhelmed by the pressures of life, often leaving them unsure of what their role in the wider society should be. What often is noticeable about Christians is not a different lifestyle but just a different belief system. What then sets a Christian apart is simply church-going and a belief in the Bible. Otherwise, the Christian appears to be little different from the average person down the street.

While this is closer to the truth, most Christians would hold that this is not the way things ought to be. For we do long to do better as we seek to serve Christ in our world. Therefore, what should set us apart is not that we have arrived, but that we are men and women of prayer. We should be characterized by humility rather than an imagined superiority.

Prayer: Lord, I long to do better, but I know I have such a long way to go. Grant that I may be marked by an openness to learn more from you. AMEN.

REFLECTION 33

FACE TO FACE:

Discovering more about ourselves

So God created man in his own image, in the image of God he created him; male and female he created them.
                                                      Genesis 1:27

To know darkness, I need to know light. To appreciate relaxation, I need to know the rigors of work. To understand something of my creatureliness, I need to have some hint about the transcendence of God. To know myself as female or male, I need to know the opposite sex.

It is in the face of the other that I come to know myself. This is an amazing and enlightening process. If I see the other merely in terms of myself, I will never truly get to know and appreciate the other person. I then simply impose my own viewpoint, values and ideas on the other. When I do this, I will not only fail to know the other, but will also fail to understand myself.

Self-understanding comes in relationship with others. It does not come in isolation. It is in the face of the other that we come to know ourselves more fully. This then involves the challenge of building relationships: learning openness, being vulnerable, learning to listen and being willing to reveal ourselves in communicating with others. This is a challenge for we sometimes find the other person daunting. But the challenge is worth taking up for it is the one way that we can truly develop and grow.

In living face to face with others we are not only encouraged and affirmed, but we can also experience the sacredness of intimately knowing someone else. Face to face we can become more aware of our particular personal gifts and qualities, as well as our blind spots and weaknesses. Avoiding the other is really hiding from ourselves.

God's purpose for our lives is that we live in reality. This means that we should be open to others and to the world around us. It also means that we are to know the Lord our God, as well as ourselves. His goal for us is that "we shall see face to face" and "shall know fully even as [we] are fully known" (1 Corinthians 13: 12). The challenge for us is to make this increasingly true in our interpersonal relationships.

Prayer: Lord, help me in my journey towards maturity to learn to be open to the love, encouragement and feedback of others. AMEN.

REFLECTION 34

PRACTICAL CHRISTIANITY:

"Walking our talk"

Is not this the kind of fasting I have chosen: to loose the chains of injustice.

Isaiah 58:6a

God is much more concerned about love, justice and mercy than with religious observance. He is pleased when the spiritual discipline of fasting is translated into practical compassion that responds to injustice, oppression, poverty and rejection (Isaiah 58: 6-7). In Scripture this sentiment is repeatedly emphasized. As far as Jesus is concerned, being reconciled to the person who is alienated from us takes priority over making an offering to God (Matthew 5:23-24). Paul reminds us that in the death and resurrection of Christ lies the implication that we can now no longer look down on or judge another person (Romans 14:9-10).

The writer of the book of Hebrews notes that God appreciates not only praise from our lips, but also our doing good and sharing with others (Hebrews 13:15-16). Zacchaeus' encounter with Christ resulted in his giving half of his possessions to the poor and repaying fourfold anyone he had cheated (Luke 19:8).

Spirituality is not simply a blissful feeling but also a practical expression. Being a Christian is not so much a state of ecstasy as it is a way of life. Our experience of spirituality is not to remain in the realm of ideas but needs to work itself out in concrete acts of love and service.

God never revealed himself as an idea but as an actor in history. He participated in the struggles of the Israelites. He sent his only Son to be among the people of his day, and he enters into the issues of our lives through his Spirit. We can do no less than "to walk our talk" and to embrace a discipleship that serves the world.

Prayer: Lord Jesus, thank you for coming among us as one who serves. Help me to partake of that same spirit of servanthood. AMEN.

REFLECTION 35

ACTIONS AND CONSEQUENCES:

Taking responsibility for our actions

A man reaps what he sows. The one who sows to please his sinful nature, from that nature will reap destruction; the one who sows to please the Spirit will reap eternal life.

Galatians 6:7b-8

Life is a basic responsibility structure. We sometimes ascribe a basic irrationality to life by thinking that what we do does not have certain consequences. We do one thing and somehow hope that something else will result. It is like planting a coconut and hoping for mangoes.

Interestingly, we tend not to have these expectations when we are doing good deeds. From good deeds we expect good results. It is when we do wrong that we hope things will not turn out too badly. And it is in this that we demonstrate our irrationality, for the law of life is none other than this: whatever we sow, we shall also reap. If we sow discord, then discord will be the result. It will hurt others and ourselves.

We are responsible for the genesis of our thoughts and the consequences of our actions. While we can thank God for the inspiration to do the good, we can not blame the Devil for the temptation to perpetrate that which is bad. For in both we are still responsible. For God's inspiration is never forced upon us but needs to be gratefully accepted, and the Devil's temptation is never so powerful that it can not be purposefully resisted.

We need to assume responsibility for our thoughts and actions. Only then can we receive God's forgiveness and the forgiveness of those we have wronged. God can and does redeem our situations but what we can not do is to excuse our wrongdoing.

Our hope that somehow things will turn out for the better is unrealistic. They will not. Negative and harmful things we have done will not just go away. They remain working as leaven in our own lives and those we influence. We need to face up to what we've done. We also need to evaluate our actions and motives. Above all, we need to be big enough to acknowledge our faults and failures.

Living responsibly is the affirmative side of the law of sowing and reaping. We can purposefully plan to do that which is right and good. In planting good seed, we affect positively the person we are becoming. We can in faith expect a good harvest.

Prayer: Lord, as I accept responsibility for my life, help me to acknowledge all that which is negative, twisted and unbecoming of my commitment to you; then help me to plan, pray and work for that which is good and right. AMEN.

REFLECTION 36

GETTING WHAT WE WANT:

God's purpose and our desires

You will be for me a kingdom of priests and a holy nation.
Exodus 19:6a

We don't always know what is best for us. But we seem to have a habit of trying to convince God and others that we want only what is best.

The Bible is full of accounts of such actions. Somewhat disturbingly, God sometimes granted his people of old what they asked for. He allowed them to practise easy divorce, although that was never his will or intention (Matthew 19:3-8). He allowed Israel to develop a most elaborate priesthood even though he wanted *all* of his people to constitute a priesthood (Exodus 19:5-6). Moreover, he allowed people in the Old Testament to have an earthly king like the other nations even though he was really their king (1 Samuel 8:4-9).

God's bending of his purposes to our demands places responsibility squarely on our shoulders. God does not push his way but seeks our co-operation and obedience. He has linked his sovereignty to our responsibility and his power to our weakness. Fortunately, he does not stop there. He continues to pursue us. He allows us the things we want and clamour for in order to make us realize that these are not necessarily for our ultimate betterment.

When some things we desire and receive go sour, we can learn the lesson of discerning the important and valuable. God can use the outcome of our second-best choices to help us to re-evaluate and search for his way and purpose. Clearly, we need to be far more careful in determining what we want. Pushing our way in life may get us to the top, but without God's blessing such achievement will be but shallow accomplishments. We can long for things, but having attained them, we may find that they are less satisfying than we expected.

Most importantly, we can have much, but if God is not at the centre of what we have, we may in fact have very little. Life's important choices need God's approval. However, should we make bad choices, this need never be the end. Repentance allows new beginnings and remarkably, God can even bring good out of our mistakes.

Prayer: Lord, help me to submit my willing and wanting to your scrutiny. AMEN.

REFLECTION 37

THOSE POWERFUL FANTASIES:
Facing our dark side

We demolish arguments and every pretension that sets itself up against the knowledge of God, and we take captive every thought to make it obedient to Christ.

2 Corinthians 10:5

Whether we are extrovert and talkative or introvert and quiet, we all at times are plagued by powerful thoughts and fantasies. Usually these fantasies have something to do with self-assertion, escapism, conquest, power and sexual gratification.

Sometimes we have thoughts that we would never carry out in real life. Even though they may seem enticing and attractive, we know that these if put into action will be hurtful to ourselves or to others. Or more specifically, we recognize that such actions are not pleasing to God and clearly go against his will.

These thoughts come as a flash and quickly disappear. At other times they linger and hang over our lives like a brooding midsummer cloud. This can both disturb and oppress us. Moreover, we become troubled, because as Christians we should not even entertain such thoughts. To blame the Devil will probably not help us much. It may, in fact, be more honest to acknowledge that we are quite capable of thinking such thoughts. That destructive, seductive and evil thoughts are somehow a part of our lives is evidence that sin is not simply incidental, but deeply embedded in our lives.

We may not be able to stop such thoughts from surfacing, but clearly we need to make sure that we do not dwell on them, nor allow them to control us. Thus we need to pray for God's protection over our minds, confess our wrong passions and fantasies, and seek the Spirit's transforming power (Galatians 5:22-23). In this way we can increasingly think about things that are true, noble, right and pure (Philippians 4:8).

Prayer: Father, you know me better than I know myself. Your Spirit is able to search the depths of my inner being. May your Spirit cleanse and purify the thoughts and intentions of my heart. AMEN.

REFLECTION 38

LESS THAN WHAT OUGHT TO BE:

Don't turn wine into water

You have planted much, but have harvested little.

Haggai 1:6a

We would like to serve as Christ served the world. That is, we would like to give what he was able to bring to humankind. And he brought so much: new life for a formalized Judaism, a new sense of God's love for all, healing for the sick, new status for women, and hope for the dispossessed.

However, we seem to be able to bring about so much less. Kierkegaard scathingly reminds us that "whereas Christ turned water into wine, the church has succeeded in doing something more difficult: it has turned wine into water." While Jesus was able to take the common and make it into something beautiful, we have so often managed to make God's beautiful gifts into something common.

Grace we have turned into law. Creativity into ritual. Spiritual ecstasy into rationality. We have made the simple difficult. We have made a caricature of the loving heart of God by making God ever so demanding. True liberation we have turned into stuffy legalism. All this we have done with great zeal and effort.

Kierkegaard's taunt is perceptive. The church has done something more difficult by turning wine into water. At least it has required greater effort. But the main task of the church is simply to cooperate with God. The church needs only to discern what the Spirit of God is doing in the world and to move in step with that. The church, in the final analysis, needs only to follow where Christ is leading. If it does this, then in many ways its task will be easy.

But when the church tries to formalize and institutionalize what God's Spirit is doing, the task becomes much more difficult. When the church changes God's agenda so that it no longer proclaims the Good News with its message of love, justice and mercy for all, then the task of the church becomes a very heavy burden indeed. For it is virtually on its own. Since God can hardly bless our agenda, we are doing the hard work of turning wine into water.

Our task is not to try to turn water into wine. Jesus does that better. Rather, our task is to carry that wine to others without changing it back to water.

Prayer: Lord, you are the source of life, of all things good, and the giver of gracious gifts. Help me to receive your grace and goodness, and help me to pass that on to others. AMEN.

FORGIVENESS

REFLECTION 39

FORGIVENESS:

The freedom to start again

If we confess our sins, he is faithful and just and will forgive us our sins and purify us from all unrighteousness.

1 John 1:9

Guilt and self-condemnation can stultify our lives. Confessing our sins and receiving forgiveness can be a wonderfully liberating experience for us. When we are forgiven we start again with a clear conscience and with lightness of step and heart. Scripture testifies to God's great generosity in his willingness to forgive. This is beautifully expressed by the psalmist: "The LORD is compassionate and gracious, slow to anger, abounding in love . . . he does not treat us as our sins deserve . . . as far as the east is from the west, so far has he removed our transgressions from us" (Psalm 103:8-12).

But receiving forgiveness can be difficult. Sometimes we find this harder than having to forgive others. It is almost as if we think that it is too easy to have our slate wiped clean. Consequently, we often do not feel forgiven and a sense of guilt lingers.

Accepting forgiveness has its cost. For forgiveness, when given so generously and received even hesitantly, places us in a special relationship with the giver—a relationship of thankfulness and responsibility.

Having been forgiven, we may no longer wallow in self-pity, nor should we hide any longer behind our guilt. We can not lightly commit the same sins again. We have been freed for new life and responsibility. And that is what is so exciting and challenging about receiving God's forgiveness. Let us move quickly to forgive so that freed we can please God and walk in his ways.

Prayer: Lord, may I learn to confess my sins in humility and not to wallow in them. Thus I can be free to serve you. AMEN.

REFLECTION 40

TANGLED RELATIONSHIPS:

The power of forgiveness

They answered, "We . . . have never been slaves of anyone."
John 8:33a

A young lady once came to see me because she was deeply troubled about her impending marriage. She was so anxious and uncertain about it that she was seriously thinking of calling it off. After exploring her relationship with her prospective husband, it became increasingly clear to me that there was no specific reason for her concern. Yet her anxiety remained. As our session drew to a close, I happened to ask her something about her relationship with her father. She exploded: "I have nothing to do with him . . . He is not aware that I am getting married . . . He is an alcoholic . . . I hate him!" Her tirade was vehement.

The story that unfolded was one of family abuse, leaving home, years without contact with family, and increasing bitterness. Quietly, she made the poignant but perceptive remark, "I think I am really afraid that my husband-to-be is going to be a drunkard like my Dad."

Here the tangled web of relationships that can so affect our lives reveals itself. My explanation to her, that bitterness binds us to the people we hate, eventually began to make sense. The thought that we impose our unresolved conflicts onto others also began to sink into her mind. But the suggestion that she should think about forgiving her father and face him again as a way of freeing herself was at that point beyond her grasp.

Fortunately, that is not where the story ended. She found grace and courage to see her Dad, forgive him and invite him to her wedding. The writer of Proverbs reminds us, "Do not say, "I'll pay you back for this wrong!" Wait for the LORD, and he will deliver you" (20:22). We think we can punish others by our withdrawal and bitterness, but we also hurt ourselves. Forgiveness sets us free and also frees the other.

Prayer: Lord, grant that I may not imprison myself in bitterness or lack of forgiveness. AMEN.

REFLECTION 41

GO AND BE WASHED:

The blessing of forgiveness and cleansing

Naaman's servants went to him and said, "My father, if the prophet had told you to do some great thing, would you not have done it? How much more, then, when he tells you, "Wash and be cleansed'!"

2 Kings 5:13

It is important that we outgrow our dependence on our parents as we move on to personal maturity. It is also important in our spiritual development that we outgrow our reliance on feelings and circumstances. Yet there are some things that we can never outgrow. We outgrow the need to be bottle-fed, but we don't outgrow the need for food. We shake off dependence upon our parents, but we don't lose the need for friendship and family. Spiritually we may outgrow a particular church or ministry, but we will always need fellowship, teaching and nurture.

But what we will never outgrow in our spiritual development is the need to be washed from our sins, shame and failure and the need to be refreshed. "Washing" is the essential starting point of our spiritual development. It is part of our entrance into the Christian life. In the book of Titus we read, "He saved us through the washing of rebirth and renewal by the Holy Spirit" (3:5b).

This inner washing from sin and guilt is symbolized by the outward washing of baptism. "Get up, be baptized and wash your sins away, calling on his name" (Acts 22:16). While water baptism is not to be repeated, inner washing from our wrongdoing and failure is to be a continuing process in our lives. We will never outgrow this need for we live broken lives in an imperfect world. But forgiveness empowers us to live lives freed for new action and service. The writer to the Hebrews suggests that "having our hearts sprinkled to cleanse us from a guilty conscience" allows us to live "in full assurance of faith" (10:22).

A simple way to remind ourselves of the need and the significance of this inner cleansing is to make a symbolic "sacrament" of our daily shower or bath. We could pray a prayer along these lines: "Lord, as this water courses over my body and washes away every spot of dirt, I claim the power of your Holy Spirit to cleanse me from everything that has been wrong, and displeasing in your sight."

Prayer: Lord, grant that I may always have the humility to come to you confessing my wrongs so that I might daily be washed and cleansed. AMEN.

REFLECTION 42

HEALING THE HURTS OF LIFE:
Christ's transforming ministry

He heals the brokenhearted and binds up their wounds.
Psalm 147:3

None of us goes through life unscathed. Others sin against us just as we sin against others. Some wrong actions against us, particularly by significant persons in our lives, can cause us deep hurt. These hurts can become festering sores and seriously affect the way we feel and act. These unresolved conflicts in our past affect our present relationships.

However, hurts can be healed. That is the good news according to the psalmist. Isaiah reminds us that the Suffering Servant does not only forgive our transgressions and iniquities but also heals our infirmities and sorrows (Isaiah 53:4-5). Moreover, the same prophet joyfully announces that the One upon whom the Spirit rested binds up the brokenhearted, comforts all who mourn, and bestows the oil of gladness instead of mourning, and a garment of praise instead of a spirit of despair (Isaiah 61:1-3).

These prophecies point to the healing ministry of Christ. It is through prayer in his name that we are released and healed from the sins and hurts that others have committed against us. We need not be shackled for the rest of our lives by negative treatment, scathing words and rejection received at the hands of others.

Christ who is the same yesterday, today and forever (Hebrews 13:8) can deal with our past as competently as he can safely manage our future. Thus we can seek his help to respond positively towards those who have hurt us, forgiving them as we invite Christ to heal us.

Prayer: Lord Jesus, I invite you to heal me where I have been hurt by the wrong actions of others so that I might be free to respond to them, not out of bitterness or disappointment, but out of the freedom of your healing love. AMEN.

REFLECTION 43

GOD OUR PROTECTOR:

Kept in the midst of life

Though he stumble, he will not fall, for the LORD *upholds him with his hand.*

Psalm 37:24

The Christian does not live in a cocoon but in the midst of life with all its complexities and dangers. We do not want it to be otherwise, for we do not want to hide or cringe from life but to participate in it in full stride. We want to grasp life with both hands and face its challenges.

This confident striding out into the world of relationships, education, business, art, politics and social involvement should never be at the cost of neglecting to pray for God's protection and blessing. For in the midst of life we need to be sheltered, sustained and nurtured. We need to be reminded regularly of God's promise that he will never leave us nor forsake us (Hebrews 13:5b).

This concern for protection was central to Jesus' prayer for us. "My prayer is not that you take them out of the world but that you protect them from the evil one" (John 17:15). This protection includes the need to be protected from ourselves. Danger does not always come from without. Sometimes it comes from within. James is aware of this fact. He reminds us that "each one is tempted when, by his own evil desire, he is dragged away and enticed" (1:

14). Thus we need God's forgiveness, protection from the Evil One as well as from our own wrong desires.

In dealing with the Evil One, we need to make sure that we do not provide him with a foothold in our lives (Ephesians 4:27). We prevent this from occurring when we deal with our inappropriate anger, unforgiveness and bitterness. But in resisting the Evil One we also need to discern the motivations of our own heart. Avoidance, fear, insecurity and the desire for power are realities we have to contend with and need to overcome. In all this we need God's protection and help. He can keep us in the midst of life with all its dangers. Even in our stumbling, struggling and being tempted, we can be kept from falling. In this God demonstrates his kindness to us. He is the rock and fortress to which we can always go (Psalm 71:3a).

Prayer: Lord, in the midst of life protect me from the Evil One and from the wrong that I myself am capable of doing. AMEN.

REFLECTION 44

THE SIMPLICITY OF THE GOOD NEWS:

Hearing its challenge and comfort

For God so loved the world that he gave his one and only Son, that whoever believes in him shall not perish but have eternal life.
John 3:16

The Bible is not always an easy book to understand. Historians, theologians and literary experts continue to struggle in understanding its origins, meaning and message. However, the Bible also has a wonderful simplicity. Humble tillers of the soil can understand its message of love, hope and liberation.

One does not need to be a biblical scholar to know that the Bible speaks of God's love for all; it offers the power of Christ to change us and the gift of the Holy Spirit to encourage and empower us. This century's great theologian, Karl Barth, was once asked at a conference, "What is the greatest thought you have ever had?" Without a moment's hesitation, Barth answered, "Jesus loves me, this I know, for the Bible tells me so."

This response captures something of the Bible's simplicity and that from a scholar who has written many weighty books on the Bible's meaning and message.

We constantly need to hear the simple messages: "Your sins are forgiven." "If the Son sets you free, you are free indeed." "You can not serve God and mammon." "The LORD is my shepherd, I shall not want." The Good News is endless. Its simplicity is staggering; its relevance amazing. Its truth is liveable; its message life transforming. The Good News touches us at the very core of our being. It challenges us to embrace God's viewpoint, diagnosis and solution for the human condition.

This, of course, is not to suggest that the Bible's simplicity is always easy to live up to. The opposite is in fact the case. To make the words of the Sermon on the Mount (Matthew 5-7) a reality in the personal and social aspects of one's life is a challenge that is frequently too much for us. We struggle to be truly forgiving, pure in our motives, generous in our attitude to others, and genuinely concerned about God's kingdom.

However, even in the midst of this struggle, the Good News is to be heard and embraced.

"There is now no condemnation for those who are in Christ Jesus."
"I will never leave you, or forsake you."
"The one who calls you is faithful and he will do it."

Thus, there is not only the challenging message of how we are to live but also the comforting good news of God's encouragement for those who struggle to carry out what God asks of them.

Prayer: Lord, may your words of challenge and comfort be light to my path and the compass to give me life's direction. AMEN.

OBEDIENCE

REFLECTION 45

THE IMITATION OF CHRIST:

The life of obedience

You became imitators of us and of the Lord; in spite of severe suffering, you welcomed the message with the joy given by the Holy Spirit.
1 Thessalonians 1:6

Jesus called men to follow him. Women were also among his disciples (Luke 8:1-3). But Jesus also sent would-be disciples home to live out their lives of discipleship among family and neighbours (Mark 5:19).

After Jesus' ascension, Christians sought to follow him, not literally, but spiritually. They sought to imitate him and live out his words.

In the history of the Christian church, what it meant to imitate Christ came to be variously understood. Some believed that we simply had to imitate Jesus' life of prayer. Others thought his obedience to the Father had to be emulated. The early church Fathers claimed that the way to truly imitate Christ was to embrace the death of martyrdom. The Franciscans held that imitating Christ involved accepting a life of voluntary poverty and adopting an itinerant life of preaching and begging. Others have claimed that it is Jesus' inner virtues of gentleness, meekness and humility that we are called to imitate. Others again, believe that it is Jesus' style of servant-leadership, his social critique or his way of relating to people that we need to emulate.

All of these responses reflect part of the truth. Today, we also need to face the question of what it means to imitate Christ. Clearly imitating Christ involves acknowledging his lordship and living in the power of his Spirit. It also involves drawing direction and inspiration from his life, words and actions for our living, priorities and projects.

Jesus is thus to be the way, life and truth for us. He should dominate our horizon, shape our thinking and direct our action. This will only come about if we acknowledge the poverty of our own ways, and search the Gospels to make Christ's words and actions relevant for our involvement in the world.

Prayer: Lord Jesus, lead me to understand your concerns, actions and involvement. Empower me to take risks in order to live by your example. AMEN.

REFLECTION 46

A MATTER OF RESPONSIBILITY:

Responding against all odds

God blessed them and said to them, "Be fruitful and increase in number; fill the earth and subdue it. Rule over the fish of the sea and the birds of the air and over every living creature that moves on the ground."

Genesis 1:28

We need to act responsibly in our world. We can not simply leave things to God or others. Yet our sense of responsibility can easily be undermined.

One frequent negative thought is that what we do as individuals does not mean much. "What difference would *my* stand make?" we ask ourselves. We need to realize, however, that seemingly small actions can have far-reaching effects. But more importantly, responsibility calls us not to be successful but to be faithful. Since in all that we do we are accountable to God (Colossians 3:17), we should be faithful even in small things (Luke 19:1-17).

Our habit of procrastination undermines responsible action. We often put off those things that are difficult or unpleasant. Yet responsibility is linked to timeliness. To be responsible means that we may need to act now regarding a particular matter. Some things cannot wait. Thus we need both discernment and the courage to act immediately when necessary.

Self-justification is a fatal "disease" that further undermines our sense of responsibility. Typical responses are: "I am doing my bit, in fact, I am doing more than my share;" and "I don't see others really carrying their load, so why should I?" What should concern us is not other people's failure but our own responsible action.

Finally, being over accommodating to others can also undermine our faithfulness in the discharge of our responsibilities. Doing a lot is not a virtue when what we *should* do gets neglected. Being responsible has to do with doing what we know we must. It also means that we should do each task at the appropriate time and with enough energy and resources to see it through to the end.

Prayer: Lord, help me to deal with the sin of procrastination; help me to do what I need to do without delay. AMEN.

REFLECTION 47

JESUS OF GALILEE:

Following in his footsteps

Whoever claims to live in him must walk as Jesus did.
1 John 2:6

The church worships Jesus as Lord and acknowledges him as seated at the right hand of the Father. In our creeds and in our confessions we proclaim that he is the divine Son of God. In hymns and oratorios we sing of his divine splendour. In our ecclesiastical art we hallow him in sacred light. So it should be. Jesus is worthy of all our adoration and praise.

However, we need to be careful that we do not replace the Jesus of history with the Christ of faith. Jesus must not become a shadowy and mystical figure for us. Jesus is the man of beard and sandal. He is also God's Anointed. Jesus is the one who ate with sinners and publicans. He was also set apart by the Father to do the Father's will. Jesus cleansed the temple. He was also the Word made flesh. He was the Father's faithful Son, yet learned obedience through the things he suffered. He was without sin, although he was tempted in all things.

It is only when we see Christ in this light that his actions and words can be a model for our involvement in the world. If we lose the human Christ by accenting only his divinity, it would be very hard to follow in his footsteps.

This does not mean that we should literally and slavishly imitate Jesus. We cannot use the context of his time. But we can try to translate what Jesus said and did into meaningful action in our day. We certainly need to take note of Jesus' response to the poor and needy, his concern to bring healing to all, his attitude towards his enemies, his lack of striving after power, and his renunciation of wealth and security.

There is so much more that we can learn as well: his method of training his disciples, his life of prayer, his way of affecting social change by starting an alternative community, his critique of the religious system.

These observations are far from exhaustive. The point ought to be obvious: the records we have of Jesus in the Gospels were relevant for the early Christian communities to shape their faith and praxis, their doctrine and life. Similarly, these records need to shape our lives as well. Let us look to Jesus, not only as the one who saves us, but also as a model for action in our world.

Prayer: Lord, help me learn from the way you lived and acted so that my life might be shaped by your example. AMEN.

REFLECTION 48

DO IT:

Taking purposeful action

Let us run with perseverance the race marked out for us.
Hebrews 12:1b

Much writing on spirituality has a search for solitude as the starting point. This is valid. New energies with which to act in life can spring forth from quietude and prayer. However, reflection can get stuck at the very start and may never issue in practical action. Thus, our spirituality loses its sense of adventure and purpose.

It is for this reason that this book focuses on action and responsibility which are more familiar to us. We usually find ourselves in the thick of life and not in some idyllic paradise. Our lives are normally busy rather than still. Instead of seeing this as a problem, we wish to affirm this reality in which we find ourselves.

While not affirming a compulsive busy-ness that drains our energy, we should celebrate our work and service, and the opportunities we have to act meaningfully. As vice-regents in God's world we are called to labour and activity. But our work should also reflect care and stewardship. It should not be exploitative but demonstrate a concern for the greater good.

Our journey of faith, which is expressed in the concerns of daily living and work, needs to be characterized by consistency and persistence. If our work is to be meaningful, we must have a sense that God is leading and sustaining us. Moreover, for work to be maintained, we must grow and develop in wisdom, courage and fortitude.

***Prayer:** Lord, in the midst of my activities, grant me wisdom and a heart that gladly obeys you.* AMEN.

REFLECTION 49

THOSE NEW YEAR RESOLUTIONS:

Discerning our life's direction

Teach us to number our days aright, that we may gain a heart of wisdom.

Psalm 90:12

Traditionally, at the end of the year we take time to reflect upon the past year, and to make new resolutions for the year ahead. When this process is superficial, it will usually amount to making statements such as, "I will spend more time with my family," or "I will try to be less reactionary," or "I will spend more time in Bible study or prayer."

The difficulty with such resolutions is that they can easily get lost in the normal pressures of daily life. The thing to do is not to rattle off some quick list of changes but to be more discerning about our whole life's direction.

We need to become aware of some key principles. First, life is purposeful. Second, our highest good is to live according to the will of God. Third, God is ready to speak to us through his Word and Spirit. Fourth, we have the responsibility to make choices.

Having affirmed these, we can ask ourselves questions: What areas in my life need strengthening? Is it my relationship with God, or family, or work, or friends? Or is it my ministry? What are some recurring difficulties in my life that I need to address? What specific commitment does God want me to make in the year ahead?

These questions move us beyond the superficial New Year resolutions that we frequently make. We begin to probe more deeply—what is really important, what is right, and what are God's priorities? We begin to touch the deeper quality of life that we are called to live; not only to do what is right, but to obey God's specific call.

The young ruler who came to Jesus was already doing right things (Matthew 19:16-21); he was already a moral person. He was keeping the commandments as he went about his duties. Nevertheless, his life lacked quality and depth. Hence, he went to Jesus with the question, "What must I do to inherit life?"

We all need to fulfill our duties. We need to work, care for our family and serve the church and the wider community. But these things do not of themselves give us the quality of life that Jesus offers us. That quality can only come by making a commitment to do "the one thing needful."

For the rich young man, the one thing needful was to sell all he had. For some of us, that one thing may be to begin trusting God in the year ahead rather than blaming him. For me, it may be to change the way I handle my finances. It may involve a rearrangement of my priorities so that I can serve God more fully in the church and the community. It may include setting time aside for intercessory prayer. It may also mean selling all that I have.

Prayer: Lord, grant that my life may be more than the endless round of fulfilling the basic necessities of life. Grant that my life may pulsate with the joy of knowing and doing your will. AMEN.

REFLECTION 50

THE MATTER OF CONSCIENCE:

Integrity within

Paul said, "My brothers, I have fulfilled my duty to God in all good conscience to this day."

Acts 23:1

We need all the help we can possibly get in our attempts to do what is right and pleasing to God. One important aid is learning to respond to our conscience. Paul states, "So I strive always to keep my conscience clear before God and man" (Acts 24: 16). In the pastoral epistles we read of the importance of "holding on to faith and a good conscience" (1 Timothy 1:19).

Conscience is nothing but our internalized set of values against which we measure our thoughts, intentions, motivations, speech and behaviour. We need to realize that conscience is not a divinely-programmed computer which automatically tells us what God's will is regarding every moral decision. If that were the case, we would have infallible guidance and wisdom.

Scripture speaks of our conscience needing to be cleansed (Hebrews 10:22). It also speaks about those with a weak conscience (1 Corinthians 8:12), a seared conscience (1 Timothy 4:2) as well as those with a clear and a good conscience (2 Timothy 1:3; 1 Peter 3:21). A weak conscience is one that is immature and over-sensitive and has not fully understood the freedom that we have in Christ.

A seared conscience is one which has become dull, ineffective and inoperative as far as the values of God's kingdom are concerned.

A clear and good conscience is what we need to develop. In the New Testament, conscience literally means "a knowing with oneself." This speaks of inner harmony and this can be achieved when our lives and actions harmonize with what we know to be right and true. In this we play a role by internalizing the truth of God's Word. As we hear God's Word and live that out in our daily lives, our internal world becomes shaped by God's concerns.

Prayer: Father, grant that my inner set of values may be constantly shaped by your Word. May I live my life with integrity based on those values. AMEN

REFLECTION 51

CHRIST'S CALL TO MOVE FURTHER:

Changing again, and again

After beginning with the Spirit, are you now trying to attain your goal by human effort?.

Galatians 3:3

Change does not come easy for most of us. Particularly not if change costs us something. One cost is that other people do not always understand when we make changes especially those that affect our job, our lifestyle, our values, our goals, or aspects of our beliefs. The changes we make are uncomfortable for them. Consequently, we may lose friends when we tread a path that they cannot understand.

Thus it takes courage to walk this new road; yet, there still lurks another danger: the greater the change and the greater the cost, the less likely we will be open to further change. This undoubtedly has to do with the tendency to attach great value to what has cost us much, more so when it carried the cost of being misunderstood.

But life cannot be lived on the basis of making only one major and costly change. We need to change continually. We see the followers of Jesus wrestling with this issue. They had left all to follow Jesus (Mark 1:16-20). Surely that was enough? No, it was not! Jesus called them to ongoing change. He called them to change their ideas, values, direction and priorities. He called them to change their perspective on power, authority, service, "childlikeness" and difficulties.

They certainly did not find that easy. And the Gospels are replete with accounts of the disciples' struggles in understanding the way Jesus wanted them to live.

No matter how great a change or sacrifice we have made at a particular time, that does not mean that we can call a halt at that point. There are further things to learn and other changes—great or small—to be made. This kind of flexibility is troublesome and disturbing, but it will certainly save us from becoming self-righteous. For the more we are aware of our sacrifices, the more they will keep us from pursuing further changes; we will have convinced ourselves that we have done enough.

Prayer: Lord, I do not find change easy, but I know it is growth-producing. Help me to be open to new things I need to learn, new changes I need to make, and new challenges I need to welcome into my life. AMEN.

REFLECTION 52

OVERCOMING OUR ILLUSIONS:
Facing life's meaning

My people have committed two sins: they have forsaken me, the spring of living water, and have dug their own cisterns, broken cisterns that cannot hold water.

Jeremiah 2:13

We were made for God, for we were created in his image. Our life is meant to find its purpose in the worship and service of God and in our obedient listening to his Word. When God is no longer the centre of our lives, then our problem is not merely that we neglect him. The problem is that we have replaced him with our own substitutes.

This is doubly dangerous. For without God's integrating work in our lives we lose our way, and delude ourselves into thinking that what we put in his place is of lasting value. We are thus double fools: we reject the real, and embrace the illusion. We suppress the truth and believe the lie (Romans 1:25).

Surely in normal life we would not walk away from a spring of water to wander thirsty into the desert, standing there defiantly to die a fool. Yet, spiritually we walk away from the spring of life, and spend the rest of our lives searching for a little water here and there, only to see it ooze away. We try this and that, but our efforts do not satisfy. We hope that something new will have all the answers, but it only leaves us with new questions. Thus we ever embark on new projects, but achieve nothing of lasting result.

Isaiah gently chides us for this folly with the words, "Why spend money on what is not bread, and your labour on what does not satisfy?" (55:2). We have to come to the stark realization that our substitutes for God's blessing, will and purpose ultimately will not work. In fact, there are times when we need to ask God to protect us from the work of our own hands. If the Lord does not build the house, then sadly we labour in vain.

***Prayer:** Lord, help me never to forsake you. But if I stray, expose what I do so that I will not hide but come into your light.* AMEN.

REFLECTION 53

HONESTY WITH DISCRETION:

Learning to share our pain

Therefore confess your sins to each other and pray for each other so that you may be healed.
James 5:6

We all need privacy—to be alone with our thoughts, to ponder on our life journey and our hopes. We need to cultivate our inner space.

Since God created us as unique beings in his image, there are some things that should be kept private between God and ourselves. Some prayers need to be prayed alone. Some struggles are ours alone. We experience grief and pain that no one else can quite understand.

Yet, we also need to learn to be open with others, particularly those with whom we share life. We need their encouragement, prayers and advice. We therefore need to learn the art of honesty with discretion.

The key to this is to build bridges of trust and understanding. This is never a quick process. We do not easily understand where other persons are coming from in the things they say. Nor do we automatically trust others. Trust is built over time in a variety of situations.

If I am with another person, not only at church but also at play or work, if we do not only pray together but also vacation together, and if we share common projects as well as meals together, then trust can grow. And where trust grows strong, it can cope with the greatest revelation and exposure. For there may come a time when there are things that must be shared, when we can no longer continue to carry them by ourselves.

Sadly, things are often shared with others when it is virtually too late. The hurt may have become a deep-seated bitterness. A continuing unhappy relationship may have become violent. Faith without answers may have turned into cynicism or despair. And failure may have begun to consume us. These are the burdens we cannot and should not bear alone. We need to learn to turn to others. But we will only turn to those whom we trust. With them, we can confess our sins, express our fears and struggles, and find solidarity in our hopes and dreams.

Prayer: Father, teach me to be quiet, waiting and reflective when I need to be, and open and trusting of others when I need to share my burdens and receive encouragement from them. AMEN.

REFLECTION 54

THE ART OF RECEIVING:

Learning to acknowledge our needs

Freely you have received, freely give.

Matthew 10:8b

We can so easily gain the idea that being a Christian is only about giving. Christians are to share God's love with others serving in ways that are helpful and being generous with their resources. But there is something that precedes giving: receiving.

We are to receive the new life offered to us in Christ. From others we receive knowledge, information, training and skills. And from those especially close to us, we receive love, comfort and affirmation. Sadly, we are sometimes not sufficiently aware of how much we do receive from others. The busier and the more important we become, the greater may be the illusion that we do not need them. But, we do. In reality, we too need to be nurtured, built up, encouraged, loved, replenished and commended.

These needs we often find difficult to acknowledge. We find it easier to give than to receive, and that is understandable. For receiving from another person tends to put us under some kind of obligation even if it is simply one of thankfulness and appreciation, while if *we* are the givers, we are in a position of strength and power. Yet we need to learn the art of receiving, as life would be impossible without it.

God understands this only too well. His first challenge to us is not to give, but that we be willing to receive: his life, his power and his direction. Only on the heels of our receiving his grace will come the challenge to also give.

Prayer: Lord, grant that I may be always open to receive from you, especially when you give to me through others. AMEN.

REFLECTION 55

THE VOICE OF THE OTHER:

Seeking advice and counsel

Let the word of Christ dwell in you richly as you teach and admonish one another with all wisdom.

Colossians 3:16a

We all would like God to speak to us directly. He sometimes does precisely that through an inner conviction, a vision or a dream. More often, he may choose to speak to us indirectly through Scripture, preaching, worship or sacrament. Or, he may wish to speak to us through another person.

The Church through the centuries has always understood the value of the spiritual guide or counsellor. Such a person is usually someone who through practical experience, suffering and reflection has learned something of God's wisdom and can thus act as our mentor.

Our contemporary world, however, seems to place little importance on such a person. We are more impressed with the medical specialist, the therapist and psychologist. We need the wise person nonetheless, although we do not need to formalize such a role. There are always those among us who have learned a little more or have journeyed a little longer, from whom we can learn and gain insight.

There are those whom we recognize as possessing gifts and abilities that we do not have. There are those who are more mature and are seen as spiritual leaders, whether they formally hold such a position or not. With such people we need to develop relationships of openness and friendship. To such we may turn for advice and direction.

This does not mean that we should become dependent on them. Other people cannot run our lives. They can not become a substitute for God. Nor can we bypass the challenge to struggle with our own life issues and to take the risks involved in making important decisions. That we have to walk the road ourselves, however, does not mean that we have to throw away map and compass. Others can provide us with advice, prayer, encouragement and confirmation.

Prayer: Lord, thank you for people to whom I can turn for guidance and encouragement. Help me to discern your voice in what they have to say. AMEN.

REFLECTION 56

ACCEPTING OUR MORTALITY:

Facing our finiteness

For since death came through a man, the resurrection of the dead comes also through a man. For as in Adam all die, so in Christ all will be made alive.

1 Corinthians 15:21-22

Death is the final intruder into human affairs. It comes to all of us. With its awesome power it calls to a halt human activity —notwithstanding all its significance and pomp, or its folly and fragility. The inevitability of death's knock at our door is usually far from our minds. We are far too busy with life and the things that seem so important. It is only when we are stricken with some illness that we have to face our mortality and begin to evaluate the motives and purpose of our busyness and existence.

Some, on contracting a serious illness, are propelled into a frantic search for healing, particularly when conventional medicine has nothing more to offer. Such a search is not inappropriate for death should be resisted, more so when its intrusion appears to be premature. (What is unhelpful is the frantic nature of such a search.) God's healing has certainly come to some but clearly not to others. The significant difference in most cases has not been a lack of faith or prayer. The difference remains shrouded in mystery.

Healing through God's intervention is never a matter of human technique nor is it under human control. Thus the search for healing can be embarked upon but healing can never be demanded nor made certain. It can only be a cry of faith in the face of mystery.

At the same time, there needs to be a recognition that it may well be time to go home. Living in the hope of the resurrection, that home-coming need not fill us with fear, and may even be a welcome prospect. In all of this, we need to recognize that our human life is ultimately fragile. We need to accept its limitations, and embrace the reality of our own mortality. Then we can cast ourselves upon the grace and promises of God.

Prayer: Lord, I am thankful for life and its continuance through your power; yet help me to know when you are calling me home. AMEN.

REFLECTION 57

BUILDING CHARACTER:

Playing a part in our development

Make every effort to add to your faith goodness; and to goodness, knowledge; and to knowledge, self-control; and to self-control, perseverance; and to perseverance, godliness; and to godliness, brotherly kindness; and to brotherly kindness, love.

2 Peter 1:5-7

It is one thing to have several jars of your favourite jam, but jam is generally spread on bread, not eaten on its own. Bread is the staple food. Jams are the extras. Similarly, we can have flashes of brilliance and bursts of enthusiasm, but we also need consistency and a sense of responsibility as the staple food of character. Spiritually, we can have times of inspiration and displays of spiritual gifts, but we also need humility, simplicity, openness, faithfulness and obedience as the staples of our spirituality.

The amazing thing in all this is that we have some say in what we become. While it is true that we have been shaped by our upbringing, have certain personalities and have gifts and abilities as well as inadequacies, this is never the whole story. We can change. We can grow. We can learn new skills. The choices we make play a very important part in our further development.

This makes life both fascinating and awesome. We are not simply biologically-determined and socially-shaped. Neither are we spiritually-determined. God does not pull the strings and we simply respond. His Spirit does not dominate but leads, teaches, encourages, challenges and pleads with us. Thus our responses are crucial and significant. In the choices we make and in the way we respond to God's Spirit within us, we play a part in becoming who we are and ought to be.

It is often the many little decisions and the small steps we take that shape our lives. The apostle Peter reminds us of this building and shaping process. He suggests that it is great to have faith, but one also needs knowledge and perseverance. It is important to be godly, but one also needs love. Brotherly kindness is a good characteristic, but one needs faith to live like that. For this development we need to assume responsibility and seek God's help.

Prayer: Lord, in the way I respond to you and make choices, may I seek to please you and do what is right. AMEN.

REFLECTION 58

SIN, THE WORLD AND THE DEVIL:

Discerning the forces of evil

As for you, you were dead in your transgressions and sins, in which you used to live when you followed the ways of the world and of the ruler of the kingdom of the air.

Ephesians 2:1,2

Sadly, wrongdoing is a part of our lives. This manifests itself in actions that are harmful to others and ourselves, and in the failure to do what is right when that is within our power to do.

Sin is not only what we do; it is also what we fail to do. Wrongdoing is not only personal; it is also instigated by the Evil One and influenced by the values of our society. This is not to suggest that we can use excuses such as: "The Devil made me do it," or "Society is at fault." James is very emphatic about establishing our personal responsibility when he writes, ". . . each one is tempted when, by his own desire, he is dragged away and enticed" (1:14).

But our personal wrongdoing is often compounded by other factors. We are personally culpable for stealing things from the workplace, but when virtually everyone does it, stealing becomes institutionalized and regarded as acceptable. The abnormal becomes normal. This compounds our own temptation to avarice.

Similarly, selfishness can become a characteristic trait of a whole society or injustice a part of its structures. This can then influence us towards wrongdoing. Thus while greed or lust is nurtured in our own hearts, Satan can stimulate those desires because we provide him with a foothold in our lives.

Paul's analysis in his letter to the Ephesians is very helpful. He reminds us that we gratify "the cravings of our sinful nature . . . following its desires and thoughts" (2:3). This clearly establishes personal responsibility, but this is aggravated by "the ways of this world," (2:2) which is societal influence. Furthermore, the reference to "ruler of the kingdom of the air' describes the negative spiritual effect of the Evil One.

As Christians who seek to do God's good in this world, we need to be aware of the ways we can become sidetracked. We need to have a healthy appreciation of the way our hearts and minds can be tempted. We all have particular points of personal weakness that we deliberately need to guard against. We also need to be aware of the influence of dominant values and behaviours in our society that do not reflect God's concern for love, justice and mercy. Finally, we need to realize that the Evil One plays his part as well. Thus, in resisting what is wrong, and doing what is right, we need to cultivate inner purity, societal awareness and spiritual discernment.

Prayer: Lord, help me to be aware of sin in its many forms and to live for righteousness. AMEN.

COMMUNITY

REFLECTION 59

EACH DOING ITS PART:

Overcoming the split-level church

Instead, speaking the truth in love, we will in all things grow up into him who is the Head, that is, Christ. From him the whole body, joined and held together by every supporting ligament, grows and builds itself up in love, as each part does its work.

Ephesians 4:15-16

Dependency in childhood is a fact of life. In adulthood, it is an undesirable state. Yet frequently, we find ourselves in circumstances which encourage dependency. The medical expert who refuses to play an educative role can leave us without options and choices. Church life can also foster dependency. This is when spiritual leaders define for us what we are to believe and how we are to live our Christian lives. While we do not want to decry the legitimate role of the expert, we do want to argue for greater participatory processes.

We need to play an active role in our own health. We also need to play a dynamic role in our own spiritual development. It is not good for us to go to church and to have everything spoon-fed to us. This creates the split-level church, with its committed core who not only do all the work but also hold all the power. Sadly, this leaves a large contingent of happy recipients, who receive the church's services but remain largely uninvolved and uncommitted.

This is not the way for us to grow and develop. We learn by doing. We grow by assuming responsibility. We develop by participatory processes where we join with others to discuss, pray, act and share.

Not only are we responsible to get information about good eating and exercise habits and then to put them into practice, but spiritually, we need to study Scripture for ourselves, read theology and serve others in order that we might grow.

If we do not become active participants, we will want more and more spiritual entertainment. This might temporarily tickle our fancy but will finally leave us bored and dissatisfied. In playing our part, exercising our gifts and assuming responsibility, we are not so much saving others but saving ourselves from stagnation and lack of dynamic development.

Prayer: Lord, thank you that you have made me in such a way that my serving and participation is a way for me to grow. AMEN.

REFLECTION 60

EMPOWERING OTHERS:
Moving from dependency to true freedom

Go home to your family and tell them how much the Lord has done for you, and how he has had mercy on you

Mark 5:19

Jesus ministered to the needy and freed them to live with a newfound hope and purpose. Some he invited to join him as part of his apostolic band. Others were sent home to get on with their normal lives. Both are equally good options. Specialized ministry and normal lifestyle are both to be qualified by the wonder of faith and the celebration of what the Lord has done for us. Both formal and informal ministry should seek to empower others. Ministry should not simply make people happy, but leave them dependent. Nor should it leave people blessed, but living in a ghetto. It should rather free men and women, so that they can get on with life in dignity and strength.

The greatest ministry that we can exercise is not simply to be charitable to others. It is relatively easy to give to others. It is also not that difficult to set up institutions of care. It is far more difficult to enable and empower others rather than simply to care for them. It is far more challenging to serve others so that they can determine their own lives than to set up institutions that foster dependency.

The most significant ministry that we can exercise is to free individuals to live life with dignity, purpose, passion and risk.

Jesus brought true freedom to the man from the region of the Gerasenes (Mark 5:1). He set him free from powerful demonic forces which had bound him in fear, degradation and isolation. But Jesus also freed him from the fear that he could not get on with life unless he stayed physically close to Jesus. The man begged Jesus to allow him to go with him (Mark 5:18). Jesus, instead, sent him home to stand on his own two feet.

This is our greatest challenge: to find ways to empower others, whether marriage partners, children as they come to maturity, employees or friends. This empowerment does not mean that a Christian becomes self-sufficient; it means that our love, friendship and expressions of care do not become stultifying and stifling. In those acts of caring we are not to be manipulative but rather seek the well-being, growth and development of the other even when that may threaten us.

Prayer: Lord, thank you that my relationship with you is based on freedom. Help me to enrich others in a way that is freeing for them. AMEN.

REFLECTION 61

THINKING KINDLY OF OTHERS:
Celebrating diversity

No one who does a miracle in my name can in the next moment say anything bad about me, for whoever is not against us is for us.
                              Mark 9:39,40

Christians are not always known for their tolerance. In obedience to Christ, we proclaim that he alone is Lord and make exclusive claims that he is *the* way, *the* truth and *the* life. Holding these beliefs, however, never justifies intolerance towards others. We should still respect people who hold different religious beliefs from our own.

It is all the more unfortunate when Christians are intolerant towards each other. We are often too quick in labelling others. "That group is too sacramental." "They are too charismatic." "She is too mystical." "That organization is only concerned about social action." "He is too liberal." Our objections can go on and on. "They hold a particular brand of eschatology." "They are too politically involved." "They are too conservative."

The reasons for differences are multiple and varied and even come down to such things as: "I do not like their pastor"; "Their worship is not exuberant enough"; "That does not seem to be a friendly church." Sadly, we have catered to these differences. One can find a church for virtually every personal preference: loud, quiet, formal, informal, liturgical, charismatic, orthodox, radical, small, large, community-based, impersonal, rich, poor . . .

Such personal preferences have now been rationalized by the sociological theory that the more homogeneous a church is, the more successful it will be. In other words, it is far easier for a group of middle class, conservative and white Christians to worship together, than to have the poor or people from other ethnic minorities mixed with them as this makes for tensions and difficulties.

Yet, that was precisely the miracle of the early church. The rich and poor, Jews and Greeks, slaves and free, and men and women were able to share a common life in Christ Jesus.

This unity in diversity did not come easily. Jesus' disciples were a pretty intolerant bunch. They were quick to dismiss anyone who did not belong to their group (Mark 9:38-41). Jesus had to teach them the finer qualities of acceptance, patience and humility. It was this same spirit of Christ which worked powerfully in the early church to bring about love and unity.

Our discipleship involves embracing the whole Christ and not simply those aspects of his ministry which suit us. Thus we need also to embrace all those who belong to Christ. This will involve being far more generous in our attitude to other Christians whose priorities and ministry concerns may be very different from our own.

Prayer: Lord, you prayed that we may all be one in love and truth. Help me to be more open, accepting and tolerant of other Christians. Help me to learn from them and work together with them for the sake of your kingdom. AMEN.

REFLECTION 62

THIS IS MY BODY:

Community as a rhythm of struggle and joy

Now you are the body of Christ, and each one of you is a part of it
1 Corinthians 12:27

We all long for a place that is truly home; a place where we are accepted and loved, where we are family, where we are safe, and where we celebrate life.

We hope that a local church might be such a place for us. Drawn together from different social and cultural backgrounds and from the busyness of our daily lives, we come together to share, pray, celebrate, love and support each other. Paul also expressed such a hope: "Consequently, you are no longer foreigners and aliens, but fellow citizens with God's people and members of God's household, . . . built together to become a dwelling in which God lives by his Spirit" (Ephesians 2:19-22).

But often our hopes are not fully realized. The local church is a human institution marked by human frailty. It is seldom a true community. It is often a place of struggle and politics.

The church is not simply the body of the resurrected and triumphant Lord; it is also the body of the suffering Jesus of Nazareth. The church is not only a divine and triumphant institution. It is much more a pilgrim community walking the difficult road of faith, obedience and service. It struggles, fails, presses on, repents and lives in hope.

In one sense, a local church is not truly home. It is more a midwife rather than our spiritual mother, a signpost rather than our destination. The local church is a companionship on the road, solidarity in the midst of struggle, a broken and incomplete life together in an equally broken world. It is a place of love in the midst of failure and tears.

To be part of a local church is not simply to find safety and security, certainly not perfection. Instead, one also finds struggle and pain. Thus we should be part of a local church, not because it is necessarily so good, but because Christ calls us into community. We remain part of that community, not because it necessarily meets all our needs, but because we can not be solitary Christians.

Prayer: Lord, I thank you that your broken body also reflects what the local church so often is. Help me to take part in the difficulty and suffering of what it means to be a church, so that I may also share in the fruit and joy that it brings. AMEN.

REFLECTION 63

THE FABRIC OF LIFE:
Faith, community and service

Therefore, as we have opportunity, let us do good to all people, especially to those who belong to the family of believers.
Galatians 6:10

The Christian life is a fabric of relationships. Most of us are not called to live the life of a solitary, but to live in fellowship: giving and receiving, and participating both in the church and in the world.

Cardinal Suenens made the observation that "a Christian is called to live out his Christian authenticity before the Lord, in the midst of brothers and sisters, in the world and in solidarity with all mankind." Here is a context where one's personal relationship with the Lord finds expression in a life together with brothers and sisters, and where that communal life exists not for itself but for the world.

With this pattern our personal life with God is not unduly dependent on the Christian community. And similarly, we do not become so drawn into our ministry to the world that the fellowship of believers becomes embarrassing or irrelevant.

Both extremes occur. Christian community can become such a preoccupation for people that it virtually becomes a substitute for their relationship with Jesus Christ. The vertical relationship thus becomes swallowed up in the horizontal. When we neglect our relationship with God, others end up carrying us. Living off other people's spirituality can only spell stagnation for us; this becomes a burden to the Christian community as well. Instead, we need to maintain the vertical relationship with Christ as well as develop a relationship with brothers and sisters.

Conversely, for others, mission to the world can be so important and all-consuming that they have little time for the household of faith. Particularly when people are working at the cutting edge of human need, the church is often seen as a cumbersome institution. However, the challenge is for our hearts to become big enough to include the church in our concerns. In the desire to do good to all, we need to include the Christian community.

Thus our rhythm of life should have God as its source and inspiration, and should find expression in the human institution of the church. And from the commonality of our life together, Christian service should radiate outwards to affect the wider society.

Prayer: Lord, grant that I may depend on you and not simply on others. May my life together with others never become an introverted ghetto but a launching pad for action in your world. AMEN.

REFLECTION 64

FREEDOM AND DIVERSITY:

Learning the art of participation

As one who is in the Lord Jesus, I am fully convinced that no food is unclean in itself. But if anyone regards something as unclean, then for him it is unclean.

Romans 14:14

One of the direct consequences of true freedom is diversity. When structures or relationships are not controlling or oppressive, diversity manifests itself as surely as nature's new growth springs up after winter. The problem with diversity, however, is that it makes things less than tidy.

In fact, coping with diversity means learning new listening and negotiating skills, learning tolerance, and seeing the others' point of view. It means having our own limited view enriched by others who see things differently. It means coming to agreement and getting involved in common projects on the basis of incorporating various perspectives. It may also mean having some of our own ideas rejected or laid aside as a result of interacting with others.

All these have implications for our marriage, family, and the way we run our churches and organizations. The tighter the control by one or several persons, the more efficient things will probably become. But things will not necessarily be richer. And it is precisely quality and richness that we should strive for, not just efficiency.

Marriage, for example, is a partnership. Both husband and wife contribute equally to its quality of life. Church is the household of faith and the family of God's people. It, too, needs to make room for all to participate and contribute to its life.

Involving others in participatory processes does not make things easier, but it will add to the genuineness of our life together. It will also add to its quality. Uniformity oftentimes becomes boring and ugly. Diversity demonstrates something of God's richness in human experience.

Prayer: Lord, help me not to be domineering in relationships. And above all, help me to genuinely open up to others' input in my life. AMEN.

REFLECTION 65

ONCE BORN AND TWICE BORN:

Celebrating differentness

I have been reminded of your sincere faith, which first lived in your grandmother Lois and in your mother Eunice and, I am persuaded, now lives in you also.

2 Timothy 1:5

God's work in nature is characterized by an amazing diversity. His work in human affairs is equally complex. While God is concerned about peoples and nations, he also cares about families and individuals. He treats us as would a Father. And since no two children are exactly the same, true fatherhood responds to individuality.

What is so surprising is that even in the common experience of conversion, God treats each one of us differently. For some this is a radical experience. Everything is turned upside down. Paul's conversion was like this. For others, conversion is a quiet unfolding of their experience of God's love within their family. Timothy certainly belonged in this category.

The Spirit of God falls suddenly on some; He wells up within the hearts of others. Some become prophets, others priests. Some have gifts of leadership, others the gift of mercy and care. Some are naturally spiritual, but need to discover Christ as its source. Others are rationalistic and they need to be spiritually changed in order to become spiritually alive.

Some seek spiritual experience, while others quietly include God in all their daily affairs. Some embrace a world-denying Christianity, while others are strongly committed to a world-affirming expression of the Christian life. Some think these differences should not be, but they are a reality. Paul acknowledges that some Christians have very different ideas about eating certain foods (Romans 14). And Jesus could quite easily cope with disciples who ministered in his name but were not a part of his apostolic band (Mark 9:38-41). This diversity calls us to be gracious towards those who are our brothers and sisters, and yet are so different.

Prayer: Lord, help me not to be threatened by Christians who are very different from me. AMEN.

REFLECTION 66

UNSUNG HEROES:

Recovering the contribution of women

There is neither Jew nor Greek, slave nor free, male nor female, for you are all one in Christ Jesus.

Galatians 3:28

We all know that the right people do not always get the credit. Life has its unsung heroes and none more so than the women in the Bible and in the life of the church. We make much of Moses, but virtually overlook the heroic stance taken by his mother and sister (Exodus 2). We know all about the apostles, but the women who supported the ministry financially (Luke 8: 3), faithfully cared for Jesus' body and were the first witnesses of his resurrection, remain shadowy figures (Luke 24). The exploits of Paul are common knowledge, but the many women who worked with him barely get a mention (Romans 16).

Some say that the Bible is a male-dominated book; there are certainly passages that can be used to denigrate the role of women. But there is much that is also liberating. Jesus formed a community of equals (Luke 8:1-3). Women were leaders of the early house churches (Romans 16:1,3, 6,12; 1 Corinthians 16:19). The Magna Carta of Christian equality (Galatians 3:28) resonates the purer heartbeat of the early church. This sought to redress the second-rate status of women in the society of that time.

This vision has implications in our view of marriage and in the role of women in the life of the church. Women are not merely extensions of their husbands. They are partners together in the gift of life. They can and should contribute equally to the life and direction of the family. They should also be able to pursue their own vocations.

In the life of the church, women can and should play a role in every aspect of its corporate life: pastoral, worship, teaching, mission and leadership. Not only am I deeply grateful for all that my wife has brought to our marriage and family, but I have also been most impressed by the contribution of women in the life of the church. That role has been not simply caring and nurturing, but also prophetic and directional. The challenge is for us men to eradicate the negative stereo-typing that is so characteristic of chauvinistic behaviour and to make room for women to become true partners in the church as a community of equals.

Prayer: Lord, grant that the men and women in the church may live beyond bigotry and stereotyping. May our church, our lives, model true partnership. AMEN.

SERVICE

REFLECTION 67

CHRISTIAN FREEDOM:
The call to servanthood

Though I am free and belong to no man, I make myself a slave to everyone.

1 Corinthians 9:19

The Gospel is the Good News. The Good News is the offer of freedom. "So if the Son sets you free, you will be free indeed" (John 8:36). Freedom is sought by those who do not possess it. That includes the poor, the sick, those imprisoned and oppressed (Luke 4:18).

Liberation is the heart of the Good News. This liberation is meant to touch the whole of our personal and social existence. It is a freedom from sin's power (Romans 6:14). It is also a freedom from the power of the law of sin and death which can only tell us what to do but cannot empower us (Romans 7). Christ's liberation, furthermore, is also a deliverance from evil spiritual forces that bring bondage and oppression (Acts 10:38) and from social structures of money, power, and ideology that can control our lives (Galatians 4:9; 2 Corinthians 10:4, 5). This surely is good news!

It is one thing to be free *from* something, but what then? What are we free *for*? That is the issue Paul addresses so clearly. Paul celebrated the wonderful freedom that Christ had brought to his life. But he was equally sure that meant that he was now a servant of Jesus Christ and of others.

To be free from sin's power as it affects us personally and socially means that we are now free to do God's will in the world. Augustine put it this way, "Love God and do as you please." What he meant was that if we truly love God, then the things we like to do will be those things that please God.

Martin Luther states it even more clearly: "A Christian is a perfectly free lord of all, subject to none; a Christian is a perfectly dutiful servant of all, subject to all." This is a difficult but challenging way to live. In fact, we may find handling true freedom more difficult than living under law and bondage inspite of its restrictions. At least our lifestyle is regulated and therefore makes us feel "safe and secure." Freedom, however, brings with it challenge, responsibility, commitment, and new possibilities which are life-giving for ourselves and others. Let us make sure we grasp this freedom that Christ offers!

Prayer: Lord, grant that the blessings and freedom you bestow on me may commit me to do your will and lead me to true servanthood. AMEN.

REFLECTION 68

MAJORING ON MINORS:

Find informal opportunities for service

And whatever you do, whether in word or deed, do it all in the name of the Lord Jesus, giving thanks to God the Father through him.
Colossians 3:17

One of the amazing lessons of life is that the things that we regard as unimportant may in fact be the most significant things that we do. Our minors may be major, and the things we do informally may be more important than what we achieve in our official roles.

Life is replete with examples. My informal and relaxing contact with my children conveyed more to them about life's values and concerns than the formal talks I had with them. My formal work in a youth welfare agency had less of a lasting impact on people's lives than the informal "ministry" of hospitality that we practised as a family. The informal work of some members of the church can have as great an impact as the formal ministry of the clergy.

What all of this means is that we should never be overly concerned with official positions and status, but be more concerned with the particular quality of life that we lead. We should attempt to live a quality of life which is open, hospitable, prayerful and caring.

Furthermore, it means that we need to be responsive to the opportunities that come our way. Thus we should not close off major areas of our lives by claiming "This is my work" and "This is my private life.' Our private lives also need to become more open and available for others. In this way interruptions become opportunities. An unexpected visit becomes a time of sharing and caring, and a chance meeting, an opportunity for building relationships. If we live this way, we may in fact accomplish more even though we may think that we are not really doing anything special.

Prayer: Lord, help me to open my whole life to the service of others. AMEN.

REFLECTION 69

DO AS GOD HAS DONE TO YOU:

Reflecting God's kindness to others

If one of your countrymen becomes poor and is unable to support himself among you, help him as you would an alien or a temporary resident, so he can continue to live among you.
Leviticus 25:35

We often think that we should treat others just as they have treated us. Consequently, we deal poorly with others because we've also been poorly treated. The challenge for us, however, is to be different. We need to learn to treat others as God has treated us.

This is the standard morality of the Pentateuch. In Leviticus 25, the Israelites were required to treat their less fortunate countrymen with generosity and kindness because the givers had been thus treated by God.

God had delivered the Israelites out of Egypt (Leviticus 25: 38) and had shown his love and care for them. Consequently, the Israelites were now to show love and care to the poor, not charging them interest on loans (Leviticus 25:35-37).

This modeling approach is almost thematic in Scripture. God forgives us; we should forgive others. God does not unfairly judge us; we should not critically judge others. God welcomes and accepts us; we should extend hospitality to others.

We could go on in this vein. But there is a complementary side to this picture; God is also tough with us. God in his generosity toward us seeks, at the same time, to help us grow into maturity and responsibility. His particular quality of goodness toward us includes his tough love approach. He disciplines us; He is kind, but also firm.

This should be the pattern for the way we treat others also. Being merely generous may in the long run make the recipient even more dependent. Being merely nice may in the long run achieve only a superficial relationship. We need to be kind, but also firm. Generous, but also responsible. Giving, but also challenging.

Prayer: Lord, you have treated me with great generosity. Help me to relate to others in the same way. AMEN.

REFLECTION 70

WITNESS BEGINS AT HOME:

Becoming what Christ calls us to be

Why do you look at the speck of sawdust in your brother's eye and pay no attention to the plank in your own eye?

Matthew 7:3

The first task of Christians is not to tell the rest of the world how it should live and conduct its affairs. It is easy to denounce violence in our society, but much harder to deal with anger in our own lives. It is easy to condemn the greed and hypocrisy that are so evident out there, while failing to be generous and consistent ourselves.

Our first task is not to be moral guardians of society: we need to preach to ourselves first, to be changed more than the world. We are the ones who need to be continually converted, to become what we already are in Christ. We shall have to work out our spirituality on the home front with some sense of integrity, for charity begins at home.

But integrity at home should not be motivated simply by the desire to keep intact our witness to others. Charity at home should be the normal expression of our practical love and care for those within our immediate sphere of responsibility. One cannot have a better apprenticeship in learning to serve the wider society than in learning appropriate responses to our parents and expressing loving care to our wife or husband and family.

When Christian values are substantially worked out in our own lives, we shall then have a basis for speaking to others. Our lifestyle shall match the message that we proclaim. Our witness to others shall acquire the "ring of truth"; we shall no longer be "hollow men," loud and moralistic on the outside, but without grace, sensitivity, generosity inside. Our witness to others shall then be an authentic expression of who we are. Our message and lifestyle have become one.

Prayer: Lord, I need to work on my "home front" before I launch out into the world. Let my love and concern be directed, first of all, to those closest at hand. AMEN.

REFLECTION 71

WITNESS AT WORK:

The art of friendship evangelism

In the same way, let your light shine before men, that they may see your good deeds and praise your Father in heaven.

Matthew 5:16

On Sundays (and also on other occasions during the week), the church is the people of God gathered together for prayer, worship, sacraments, teaching and fellowship. During the rest of the week, the church is the people of God scattered in the home, school and workplace. In our neighbourhoods and places of employment, we can maximize our contact with people who may not be part of the Christian community.

Having been employed in various work environments, I am always struck by the varied witness of Christians in the workplace.

Some Christians make such a distinction between their church life and their work life that God, so to speak, is left at home. Nothing in their speech or actions marks them out as Christians.

Others take a moralistic stance. They tend not to join in the snack time or lunch break and social activities of the workplace, but are quick to reprimand people on their swearing and dirty jokes. They generally come across as moral guardians and are not particularly liked by their work colleagues.

Some others, and sadly these appear to be in the minority, display a level of engagement with others that is winsome and exemplary. Some of the characteristics of this approach are: a high level of normal social contact, taking a helping interest in specific persons, personal attitudes of fairness and justice, genuine interest in the welfare of the company or business, and personal qualities of realism and joy.

Invariably, such Christians are not only respected, but are also approached for help and advice. It is often while serving others that we get the opportunity to share something of our faith and commitment to Christ. Thus the prim-ary issue in the workplace is not what we should say, but that we should live out a quality of life that would set the stage for what we shall say later.

Prayer: Lord, help me to be sensitive to the needs of people in my workplace. Let me befriend individuals and minister to them in ways that are appropriate. AMEN.

REFLECTION 72

DESPISE NOT THE DAY OF SMALL THINGS:

Growing into greater responsibility

*The L*ORD *God took the man and put him in the Garden of Eden to work it and take care of it.*

Genesis 2:15

Many of us, particularly those with some drive and ambition, have certain ideas about what we are good at and could accomplish in the world. We need to realize, however, that we do not immediately come into places of position, authority and influence. We have to undergo long periods of training and preparation first. This is just as well; power and position without wisdom and humility are potentially dangerous—dangerous not only for others, but also for ourselves.

Moses had to have some careful retraining in God's "school of the desert" before he was ready to step onto the stage of history with the great Exodus event. Such retraining is often difficult for us. We find it hard to accept the gap between what we know we can do and what we have been assigned to do at the present time.

This interim period can lead to a lot of frustration. It causes some to despise the present and grasp for the future, with its hoped for position and influence. That, however, is precisely the temptation we need to resist. For despising the present with its more mundane cares and responsibilities ill equips us for the bigger and better things that lie ahead. We need to grow by endowing our mundane responsibilities with purpose and significance.

Adam and Eve were given the awesome task to "fill the earth and subdue it" and to rule over the animal kingdom (Genesis 1: 28). But their apprenticeship for this task started by having to care for a garden. What they did or did not achieve there was to have ramifications for the execution of the greater task.

Similarly, our vision of those greater things that we can and should do will always be restricted by our obedience in the small things that we need to do now.

Prayer: Lord, I want my life to be fruitful and significant. Help me to grow in strength of character now so that I may later exercise greater responsibility with grace and dignity. AMEN.

REFLECTION 73

HAVING AND NOT HAVING:

Learning the art of detachment

From now on . . . those who buy something [should live] as if it were not theirs to keep; those who use the things of the world, as if not engrossed in them.

1 Corinthians 7:29-31

Christians are to live in the real world of politics, business and work. These things are not to be shunned simply because they throw up all kinds of ethical questions and problems. The world of politics, business and work is never without its moral dilemmas. While issues are often complicated, grey and blurred, it is in the real world that we need to function as Christians with values such as justice, love and mercy.

What ought to be clear is that our work must not consume us. But that is far from easy. The more important the position we hold, the more likely it will control us. Therefore we need to learn the lesson of inner detachment. This involves being fully committed to what we do, without making that our ultimate value or our final priority.

Detachment can help us to get the things we are doing into truer perspective. Our work should never be the sum total of our lives. We have also responsibilities to family, friends and neighbours. Our work, moreover, can never have ultimate value for it will always be marked by human error, sin and selfishness. Therefore our work must not be identified as totally reflecting the kingdom of God.

Moreover, detachment will help us to discern more clearly the ethical issues that are involved in what we do. The more we are caught up in something, the more blinded we are likely to be. Some distance will allow us to re-evaluate and then we shall be able to make better choices.

Paul reminds us that this present world is passing away. This means that the world we are making through our labour will not last forever. Therefore, we need to make sure that what we have, make, produce, engineer and develop is not the sum total of what we are.

Prayer: Lord, thank you for the abilities you have given me for work and productivity. Help me not to lose myself totally in those important pursuits. AMEN.

REFLECTION 74

A NEW CREATION:

Realizing our potential

Therefore, if anyone is in Christ, he is a new creation; the old has gone, the new has come.

2 Corinthians 5:17

We Christians are set apart by our beliefs. We believe that God created the universe, that he is involved in human affairs, and that through Christ he has shown his love for humankind. This view is not held by many other people.

But it is one thing to have a different belief system, and another to have a quality of life that is different from other people. Are we more balanced, integrated and mature than others? Are we more committed to love, justice and mercy? Are we more stable, resilient, stronger in character and reliable? Do we demonstrate greater sensitivity in relationships, in family life, marriage and parenthood? Are we free from fear and anxiety? Do we Christians enjoy physical, emotional and social well-being more than others?

These are difficult questions. We know our weaknesses. We have also met non-Christians who are exemplary in their personal qualities. So what difference then does Christ really make in us? Clearly, we Christians do not have it all together for we are not perfect. We have struggles and weaknesses just like any other.

The difference lies not so much in what is actual, but in what is potential.

Christ works in our lives by his Spirit. Our obedient response to his Spirit makes ongoing change and growth possible. We can grow in the fruit of the Spirit (Galatians 5:22, 23) and in wholeness and integrity (1 Thessalonians 5:23). The challenge for us is to take hold of what we already have in Christ (Colossians 2:10) and to go through the learning experiences of life so that we may grow in wisdom, holiness and service.

***Prayer:** Lord, help me to draw more deeply on the life and inspiration that you offer so that I might grow into the fullness of life you have for me.* AMEN.

JUSTICE

REFLECTION 75

BE ANGRY, BUT SIN NOT:

A passion for justice

"In your anger do not sin": Do not let the sun go down while you are still angry and do not give the devil a foothold.

Ephesians 4:26,27

Anger is a normal human emotion. There are situations where anger is appropriate, particularly where there is injustice.

Jesus expressed anger at the death of Lazarus (John 11:33,38). While our Bible translations weaken the power of his emotions by recording that "Jesus was deeply moved," in the original Greek text it states that he "snorted in anger and displeasure." Jesus may well have been angered by the brokenness of our world and the reality of death.

The Bible also speaks about God's anger. While God "is gracious and compassionate, slow to anger and rich in love" (Psalm 145:8), he frequently expressed his anger to an unrepentant Israel (Judges 2:20, Isaiah 5:25).

Our anger, however, is often for the wrong reasons. We get angry because we are intimidated, misunderstood, falsely accused, or mistreated. Worse, ours is often the anger of reaction because our dignity has been offended. Worst, our anger is sometimes displayed because we do not get our own way. We thus retaliate or seek revenge. Anger in these circumstances is sinful and destructive;

it is also selfish. James reminds us that this "anger does not bring about the righteous life that God desires" (James 1:20).

Jesus was angry at Lazarus' death. But he was not angry when there was a threat to his own life. "When they hurled their insults at him, he did not retaliate; when he suffered, he made no threats" (1 Peter 2:23). While Jesus was angry because of hurt to his friend, we are often angry because of hurt to ourselves. This anger only leads to retaliation and possible bitterness. Jesus' anger led him to prayer and positive action on behalf of his friend. It is only when our anger is focused on injustice done to the other that we do not sin. When this leads us to prayerful and constructive action on that person's behalf, anger has been a positive emotion.

Prayer: Lord, help me to learn to act on behalf of others when they have been unjustly treated, but teach me to commit into your hands injustice done to me. AMEN.

REFLECTION 76

CRY FREEDOM:

A ministry of transformation

Blessed are those who mourn, for they will be comforted
Matthew 5:4

Christians in North America and Europe seem preoccupied with concerns that are very different from those in Asia, Africa and Latin America. Those in the West search for meaning and happiness while they already have so much. Those in Asia, Africa and Latin America cry for freedom even though they have so little. Their cry, however, is also to become our cry—not simply because we need to stand in solidarity with them regarding the oppression and exploitation that they are experiencing, but because we, too, are in bondage. While our bondage is often due to our selfishness, it ought to be due to something else, namely, a sense of common responsibility. If I am free but my brother or sister is not, then I am not truly free. If I have enough but others live in need, then I too live in deprivation.

That is why Christians can never be truly happy in this world. For whatever we may receive of God's love and grace, and whatever blessings come from our life together as Christians, we will always live with the thought that others live in deprivation, fear and rejection.

That cannot but affect us and we dare not turn a deaf ear. For if the cry for justice reaches the ear of God, it also needs to reach our hearts.

Thus, whatever joy we may have here, such joy will always be mixed with sadness, for we can never exclude from our hearts the pain and suffering of others. Luther translated the familiar words from Matthew as "Blessed are the sorrow-bearers for they shall be comforted." As Christians, we do need to carry the sorrow of others, and that can lead us to prayer and fruitful action.

David Wilkerson in *The Cross and the Switch-blade* tells how his heart was burdened as he walked the streets of New York. The heartcry of the gang kid and the drug addict became his heartcry. When our lives are touched by human need, we can never be happy or free until others share the freedom and joy of wholeness in Christ.

Prayer: Lord, give me a heart big enough to include the cry and need of others. AMEN.

REFLECTION 77

SEEING TRULY:

Going beyond caricatures

The poor man and the oppressor have this in common: the LORD gives sight to the eyes of both.

Proverbs 29:13

We often see only what we want to see. We find it hard to acknowledge that one of our children is drifting toward disaster, or we are unable to see the signs of serious illness in one of our loved ones. We tend to repress unpleasant things.

Moreover, we approach all of life from our particular point of view. We are all one-sided. We are all rooted in particular traditions and these influence us to think and see things in particular ways. One of the challenges of living is to increasingly incorporate others' perspectives into our own. This not only enriches us, it can also make for a more just world.

The poor man and the oppressor have nothing in common. One is a victim of the other. The writer of Proverbs notes, however, that both have the ability to see. But sadly, often they see only from their own perspective. The rich see the poor as lazy. The poor see those in power as oppressive. And to extend this further, men tend to see women as subservient to their interests. Whites hold blacks in disregard. Youths think little of their parents. Bosses and workers are frequently suspicious of each other. Yet this kind of seeing is often in terms of caricatures and stereotypes.

We need to learn to see people and things as they really are if we are to build a more just world. For this we need a spirit of wisdom and understanding so that we can judge not simply by generalizations, or reactions, but judge righteously (Isaiah 11:2-4). The only way to come to that kind of understanding is to enter the world of the other. We do that by building relationships, opening our hearts and careful listening. In building these bridges, we often discover that the other was not quite what we had first thought. Then we discover the real world and begin to see more truly.

Prayer: Lord, forgive me for the many times I have made generalizations about other people and have thus misjudged them. Grant me the spirit of wisdom so that I may see others in the light of love and thus see them truly. AMEN.

REFLECTION 78

THE GREATEST GOOD TO THE LEAST DESERVING:

Living the upside-down kingdom

On the contrary, those parts of the body that seem to be weaker are indispensable, and the parts that we think are less honourable we treat with special honour.

1 Corinthians 12:22-23a

When one reads the New Testament carefully, one cannot but be impressed by its very different vision of life. It almost seems as if things are upside-down. Sinners rather than the "righteous" are justified. The rich are sent away empty-handed. The outcasts of society are welcomed to the banqueting table. Despised minority groups such as the Samaritans are held up for their exemplary behaviour. Those that the law demands to be punished are forgiven. The poor are called blessed, and the strong are the weak. It is all so different to what we would normally expect.

Our values suggest quite the opposite. The rich sit at the feasting table. The "good" succeed. Those that are socially acceptable are held up as deserving respect and emulation. The strong win, and the weak are downtrodden.

Some say that Jesus' ethic and vision of life was naive; certainly unworkable in our complex and pragmatic society, they claim.

Others believe that Jesus' ethic was only for the interim. It was for those awaiting the appearance of the kingdom of God in its fullness. It has no relevance for us who live in an age after the kingdom "failed" to arrive.

The challenge for us, however, is to take these seemingly upside-down ideas of Jesus seriously and attempt to live them out. Peace and reconciliation can achieve greater good than anger and retaliation. Serving the weak enriches the *server*, and God's wisdom is often with the childlike and humble, rather than with the proud and ostentatious.

It is important to remember, however, that living by the words and actions of Jesus will not necessarily mean success. At least not in the way we normally measure it. Instead, success is learning to live in the hope that while you appear to be losing, you are in fact gaining ground. It is believing that in the struggle of learning the art of relinquishment, you are receiving all things.

***Prayer:** Lord, may my desire for safety, security, and respect be transformed by the adventure of faith that takes the risks that lead to life and justice.* AMEN.

REFLECTION 79

CITIZENS OF THE KINGDOM:
The lordship of Christ over all of life

Give everyone what you owe him: If you owe taxes, pay taxes; if revenue, then revenue; if respect, then respect; if honour, then honour.
Romans 13:7

The Christian is a member of the Christian community. The Christian is also a public citizen. The Christian belongs to God's kingdom, but is also a member of society.

But the Christian can not separate life into two spheres: the sacred and the secular. Finally, we are citizens of only one kingdom, God's, and it is his kingdom that we should seek to live out in this world.

Martin Luther unfortunately didn't get that quite right and separated the personal and the public spheres of the Christian's life. He wrote, "Do you want to know what your duty is as a prince, or a judge, or a lord, or a lady with people under you? You do not have to ask Christ about your duty. Ask the imperial or the territorial law." Luther continues, "When a Christian goes to war or when he sits at a judge's bench punishing his neighbour, or when he registers an official complaint, he is not doing this as a Christian, but as a soldier or a judge or a lawyer."

What Luther seems to be saying is that in the personal sphere of life, one must find out what Christ wants, but in the public sphere, one must do what the state says. Clearly, life can not be divided like that. In the public sphere of life, the Christian is also to ask, "What does Christ want me to do?"

In this sense, we are citizens of the one kingdom: God's. We are called to live out God's values in the whole of life: in the personal and the public, in the sacred and the secular.

This means that church and world, and family and work are all to be influenced by Christ. It means that in our involvement in society, we must seek to live out the values of God's kingdom within the context of the kingdoms of this world. This means that our role in society is to be a Christian response that seeks to bring about transformation.

It is not always easy to know what a distinctly Christian response might be, but the broad parameters are clear: freedom, justice and mercy for all. This is to characterize the church as much as the government, family life and the workplace. The challenge is to bring every aspect of our life under the lordship of Christ.

Prayer: Lord, while I deeply appreciate the gift of life and salvation you have given me, I often want areas of my life to be autonomous. Help me to appreciate your rightful lordship over the whole of my life. AMEN.

REFLECTION 80

WHAT IN THE WORLD IS WORLDLINESS?

Resisting the powers

Do not conform any longer to the pattern of this world, but be transformed by the renewing of your mind.

Romans 12:2

Some Christians understand worldliness as having to do with certain kinds of behaviour such as dancing, smoking or going to the movies. In an earlier era, worldliness was characterized as engaging in certain forbidden activities on the Sabbath such as work, sports or games.

For some, worldliness is even more narrowly defined and has to do with avoiding any unnecessary association with non-Christians. This, in effect, defines Christian virtue as withdrawal from life.

For many others, worldliness is usually cast in terms of personal morality. Often, this means that worldliness has to do with a lack of appropriate values regarding sexuality, but morality is much wider. All these perspectives on worldliness are, however, totally inadequate.

The New Testament uses the word "world" in four ways: all of created reality (i.e., this entire universe); this particular globe that we call earth; the world of people (i.e., humanity in general); and the world as a value system opposed to God.

When the Bible says that we are not to "conform to the pattern of this world," it means the "world" as a *value system opposed to God.* It has nothing to do with withdrawal from social contact with other people.

Paul makes that point very strongly: "I have written to you in my letter not to associate with sexually immoral people—not at all meaning the people of this world who are immoral, or the greedy and swindlers, or idolaters. In that case you would have to leave this world" (1 Corinthians 5:9-10). Paul was concerned about discipline within the church, not withdrawal from life.

Thus, Christians are different from others, not so much in terms of dress or general social behaviour, but in living according to a very different set of values. These values not only concern morality and sexuality. They also include our attitudes towards possessions, power and status. They have to do with peace-making, forgiving our enemies, justice and serving others.

Worldliness has to do more with domination than service; indifference rather than loving regard for the other; materialism and selfishness rather than generosity and hospitality; and idolatry and the demonic rather than that which is godly.

The world seeks to weave a pattern of meaning for our lives through its various ideologies and values; we must discern where these are not in consonance with God"s kingdom and not be afraid to reject them in our lifestyle.

Prayer: Lord, you have not left the peoples and governments of this world without the marks of your grace. Help me to discern what belongs to the general good and is in harmony with your Word. But help me to reject those values that are not of your kingdom. AMEN.

REFLECTION 81

THE WITNESS OF THE PAST:

We can transform our world

You are the salt of the earth.

Matthew 5:13a

There are things in the past that Christians need to be ashamed of. The crusades, the power-hungry church of the Middle Ages, and the linking of Christian mission with colonialism are but a few examples where the church failed to be light and salt to the world.

Yet there is also much that we can be thankful for and that can inspire us. The historian Edward Gibbon in his famous book, *The Decline and Fall of the Roman Empire*, points out that one reason why the Christian church survived the collapse of the pagan Roman state was because it had become a significant social force characterized by benevolence.

The great German scholar, Adolf Harnack, in his *The Mission and Expansion of Christianity*, demonstrates that the early Christian communities showed care for widows and the sick, checked infanticide, founded asylums for the young, encouraged care of slaves, and opposed the wanton bloodthirstiness of gladiatorial events. And W.E.H. Lecky, in his *History of European Morals*, states that Christianity was a movement of "philanthropy which has never been paralleled in the pagan world."

The monastic movement in the Middle Ages did much in the area of education and agriculture. Major social projects followed in the wake of the Wesleyan revival in England including the abolition of slavery. There have been also the outstanding work of the Quakers, the Moravians, the Salvation Army, the YMCA, World Vision and Mother Teresa.

Yet it is not only when the church has been an instrument of compassion in the world that it has had a salting affect. This has also come about when it has been committed to social justice. It might be of interest to quote from Albert Einstein's letter to the *New York Times*, December, 1940:

> as a lover of freedom, when the revolution (Nazism) came to Germany, I looked to the universities to defend it (freedom). . . . But no, the universities were immediately silenced. Then I looked to the great editors of the newspapers . . . they, like the universities, were silenced in a few weeks. Only the church (Confessing church) stood squarely across the path of Hitler's campaign for suppressing truth. I never had any special interest in the church before, but now I feel a great affection and admiration for it. . . . I am forced to confess that what I once despised, I now praise unreservedly.

The challenge for us in all of these is that we need to be concerned not only about caring for the weak in our society, but also in being resolute in our concern for justice.

Prayer: Lord, save me from a selfish life that has no room for compassion and no vision for justice. AMEN.

CELEBRATION

REFLECTION 82

JOY IN EACH MOMENT:

Enjoying the present

Surely goodness and love will follow me all the days of my life.
                                                        Psalm 23:6a

We can live as if the best always lies in the future. This is not wholly inappropriate. God may well have some good things in store for us. But the best can also lie in the present. In fact, there are many good things that we need to appreciate now, for they will never come again.

The wonder of childhood discoveries is unique to that time in our life. The security of being tucked in bed and have stories told and prayers said is not experienced when we are adults. The startling amazement of becoming aware of one's own body and one's sexuality, and the bewilderment and excitement of first love are unique experiences.

There are many other important experiences. The energy of adolescence. The adventure of starting life together with another person. The miracle of watching a fetus grow in the womb of its mother and the sheer joy of its birth. The challenges and joys of parenthood. The wisdom of old age. These are all nonrepeatable passages of life.

Many of our spiritual experiences are similarly unique. The stumbling nature of our first prayers. The emotional excitement of receiving Christ into our hearts. The first hesitant attempts of sharing with others the good news of what God has done in our lives. The thrill of discovery that God actually provides and cares for us. The adventure of beginning to work for God in ways that help other people. We could go on but the point should be abundantly clear. We go through unrepeatable stages in our physical, social, intellectual and spiritual development. These events need to be appreciated for what they are. In them we need to see God's special involvement and care.

We thus need to celebrate at the particular time what we have been given. It is surely those who enjoy the journey who will not be left with recriminations at journey's end. This does not mean that everything will be easy along the way as no journey is without its pitfalls and difficulties. But such experiences only help us appreciate the good and the beautiful. The joy, therefore, is as much in the journey as in the destination.

Prayer: Lord, grant that each stage of my life may be marked by your grace and blessing, and by my appreciation. AMEN.

REFLECTION 83

THE REALITY OF A TWENTY-FOUR-HOUR DAY:
Prioritizing for God's glory

So whether you eat or drink or whatever you do, do it all for the glory of God.

1 Corinthians 10:31

In our highly urbanized and industrialized centres of population, we experience a good deal of fragmentation. We are constantly torn by the demands of home and family, work and education, and our wider interests, be they political, cultural, church or service to the community.

Because of these pressures, we have to prioritize and thus may run the risk of forcing important things off our agenda. Moreover, we are also under tremendous pressure to specialize. Work, ministry, even a creative hobby, or a particular form of leisure activity may demand increasing amounts of time and energy if we are going to be successful. The challenge in all of these is that by focusing on a particular activity, we may become expert in that field and enjoy the benefits that accompany such success. The pressing question however is: At what cost? What do we leave un-done in order to succeed? What do we relegate down the priority list in order to accomplish major projects? Do we forego friendships? Do we minimize time with our family? Do we neglect the cultural side of our lives? Have we still time for simple chores? Is Christian service to be passed on to someone else?

In wrestling toward some answers, several guidelines suggest themselves. The first is that we should strive for holism. The spiritual, intellectual, family, social, vocational and cultural aspects of our lives all need development. This means that we cannot so major on one aspect of our lives that the rest is neglected. Secondly, we should aim for simplicity. Specialization should be complemented by a willingness to perform the simple tasks of life. Servanthood, justice and care can become central themes that reflect themselves in all we seek to do. And finally, we should aim for realism. Thus, we need to work within the limits of our abilities and resources.

Important in our search for answers is gaining a sense of God's direction for our lives, and the realization that his will does not run counter to fulfilling our basic responsibilities in all areas of life.

Prayer: Lord, grant that all my priorities in life be not self-serving, but spring from a desire to serve others particularly those within my sphere of responsibility. AMEN.

REFLECTION 84

IN EVERYTHING:

Experiencing God's providential care

His divine power has given us everything we need for life and godliness through our knowledge of him who called us by his own glory and goodness.

2 Peter 1:3

For most of us, needs and wants get a little mixed up. We do not always need what we want. But our needs are more than the basic necessities of life: food, clothing and shelter. We also need meaning, purpose, life goals, work and friendship. The list could go on. Some would want to add education, prestige and money. For some the list is endless. They hold a position of triumphalism. They believe that a Christian can have everything, because in Christ all things are ours. They conveniently forget that God's way includes suffering and relinquishment.

Equally important, we must never forget that we always stand in relation to others. Our needs and certainly our wants cannot be isolated from the needs of our brothers and sisters in Christ and our neighbours. For everywhere we encounter the neighbour in whose face we read the reminder of Jesus: ". . . whatever you did for one of the least of these brothers of mine, you did it for me" (Matthew 25:40).

Scripture asserts the reality of God's providential care. It promises provision for our needs. That provision is not only for our spiritual needs; it is also for all our life as we experience it in all its dimensions. But Scripture also strikes a note of sobriety. Agur prays: "Keep falsehood and lies far from me; give me neither poverty nor riches, but give me only my daily bread. Otherwise, I may have too much and disown you and say, "Who is the Lord?" Or I may become poor and steal, and so dishonour the name of my God" (Proverbs 30:8-9). Agur reminds us that there is something more important than having much or little, and that is to honour and trust God. In the letter to Timothy the same sentiment is emphasized: "Command those who are rich in this present world not to be arrogant nor to put their hope in wealth, which is so uncertain, but to put their hope in God" (1 Timothy 6:17).

We are thus challenged to trust God for our needs: spiritual, social, economic and relational. We also need to see life as sustained by God and not as the result of our own achievements. We need to celebrate what we have and not to envy others. And that whether we have much or little, we need to demonstrate a generosity to others that is part of our thankfulness to God.

Prayer: Father, thank you for what you have given me. May I in turn be as generous to others as you have been to me. AMEN.

REFLECTION 85

STRENGTH IN THE MIDST OF WEAKNESS:

Experiencing God's sustaining care

For when I am weak, then I am strong.
2 Corinthians 12:10b

We sometimes wrongly think that being a Christian means that everything will always work out and that all our problems will be solved. We think that we can always be strong and in control. Yet we soon discover otherwise. Life throws up its contradictions and we can be overwhelmed by its difficulties. The secret of the Christian life is not that we are always strong, but that in the midst of anguish, despair and difficulty, we can discover God's grace and participation.

Difficulty does not mean that God has abandoned us. Rather, difficulty challenges us to learn from these experiences and grow through them. This is far from being an easy lesson. For we usually think that we should be able to manage by ourselves; not to do so would reflect poorly on our abilities. To suggest that we can not always achieve this is not to make a virtue out of weakness or inability. If success is not always achievable, then equally, weakness and failure need not be the norm of our lives.

The apostle Paul experienced weaknesses, insults, hardships, persecutions and difficulties (2 Corinthians 12:10). He did not seek them; he, in fact, tried to get away from them (12:7).

But one cannot always so easily avoid difficulties. Some we have to go through, particularly, those which are not of our own making.

It is at these points in our lives that we need to learn the art of abandoning ourselves to God. Christ cast himself into God's care at his crucifixion. He experienced in that abandonment the resurrection. We can do no other. We can also come to experience God's power made perfect in our weakness (12:9). The difficulty is that we often want to carry our struggles alone rather than invite God or a caring friend into our circumstances. When we are sustained in our difficulties, we cannot only persevere, but we can also be thankful.

Prayer: Lord, help me not to be so independent and foolish as to exclude you from my pain and struggles. Help me to open myself to your sustaining strength and grant me the power of your grace. AMEN.

REFLECTION 86

LET US

Building life together

Let us not give up meeting together . . . , but let us encourage one another.

Hebrews 10:25

Loneliness and isolation can harm or hinder our development as persons. This forms one extreme on a continuum. The other extreme is to live in communities or "holy enclaves" where relationships become very dependent. Since God's call is for us to share life with one another, neither isolation nor dependency are the ideal, but participation and celebration.

Relationships are to be freeing and growth producing, not stifling or narrowing. This theme of participation and encouragement is central to the writer of the Hebrews. He calls us to a common involvement. "Let us draw near to God" (10:22). "Let us hold unswervingly to the hope we profess" (10:23). "Let us consider how we may spur one another on toward love and good deeds" (10:24). "Let us not give up meeting together . . . but *let us* encourage one another" (10:25). In the emphasis on "let *us*," the writer stresses the importance of Christians doing things together.

We need to meet together for prayer, worship and teaching. We also need to learn to share together in other aspects of our lives. To achieve this common life, we clearly need to make room for each other. A quick personal prayer is much easier to engage in than corporate prayer. It is usually quicker to do things ourselves than to involve others. However, despite the hassles of community life, the fact remains that we do need one another. In our solo efforts we can easily become self-centred, discouraged or sidetracked. In doing things with others, we are not only sustained but also enriched.

Prayer: Lord, teach me what it means to journey together with my brothers and sisters. I open my life to others' participation and involvement. AMEN.

REFLECTION

REFLECTION 87

IS OUR SPIRITUALITY BIG ENOUGH?

Moving beyond our structures and systems

As the heavens are higher than the earth, so are my ways higher than your ways and my thoughts than your thoughts.

Isaiah 55:9

Peter thought he knew Jesus very well. But his vision of Jesus was too narrow. It did not foresee Jesus' suffering, death and resurrection (Mark 8:31-33). Like Peter, we often think that we have our Christian life all worked out. We have formulated certain criteria by which we measure our spirituality. For some, these have to do with right doctrine. For others, with having certain spiritual experiences. Still, for others, with being involved in certain issues of social concern.

The danger in having such formulations is that if we fulfill the criteria we have established, we become smug and self-righteous. Even worse, we begin to rely for comfort and security on our man-made systems. Jesus had to change Peter's perceptions, and he has to shake us loose from the systems that we create.

The Christian life is more than living up to a set of rules. It has to do with our relationship with God and our neighbour (Matthew 22:37). It has to do with a whole way of life (John 14:6). It cannot be reduced to neat and tidy categories. Consequently, we need to become open to move beyond the familiar, to question the criteria and categories that we establish, and to invite the Spirit to disturb us. Let us not be too quick in assuming that we have it all worked out and that our programs are God's.

Isaiah's sober reminder is that God's thoughts are not our thoughts, neither are our ways his ways (55:8). Therefore we continually need to entertain the question, "Lord, is my spirituality big enough to include all your concerns for the world?"

Prayer: Lord, I can only catch a glimpse of the fullness of your purposes. I have but a limited grasp of who you are and what you can do. Save me from so limiting Your concerns that I misconstrue your intention for me, for the church and for the world. AMEN.

REFLECTION 88

THESE RESTLESS HEARTS OF OURS:

Seeking the good

He has also set eternity in the hearts of men.

Ecclesiastes 3:11

We are the crown of God's creative activity. Made in God's image, we partake of all that is good and beautiful. But we are also scarred by the results of our own willfulness, anger and sin. We are thus tragic figures in a universe where meaning and purpose often elude us. We can understand and see, but we can also be deluded and blind. We are capable of great good, but human history bears the marks of our great follies as well.

Thus we are torn. We know the good, but do not always perform it. Our highest aspirations are not always realized, and our finest dreams can become nightmares. Nevertheless we continue to strive for the greater good. We do not accept that the worst is all we can expect. We will not acquiesce to the triumph of evil.

Powerful impulses stir us to hope for that which we can barely grasp, the shadowy outline of that which we can only vaguely discern. That impulse springs not from our own heroic nature or our unselfish longing for the better. It comes from the shaping hand of God's wisdom. He has set eternity in our hearts, limited though we are by our humanity and history. Marked by God's hand, we are restless in searching for the good.

We strive and struggle. We hope. We pray. With the touch of this invisible Hand which shapes us more than the environment around us, we can be more than the sum total of our circumstances. We can press forward and live beyond the here and now.

God's eternity in our hearts is our glory. It makes us long for the better. It inspires hope. Yet it can also make us sad for it reminds us of that which ought to be but has not yet come to pass. However, in this sadness we can find a way to prayer which will empower us to new action and responsibility.

Prayer: Lord, thank you that you have made me in such a way that there are constant impulses in me seeking the good and the better. May my restless heart seek your power and your way in the realization of those desires. AMEN.

REFLECTION 89

ACCEPTING LIMITATION:

Discovering the second law of spirituality

The eye cannot say to the hand, "I don't need you!"
1 Corinthians 12:21

Watchman Nee claimed that the first law of spirituality has to do with the exercise of the gifts God has given us, and the second law with accepting personal limitation. The latter does not deny our need for continued growth and development. It simply acknowledges that we cannot know and do everything. It is not an argument against developing new skills and interests; it simply suggests that we all approach life from a particular perspective, interest and concern. From there, we make our particular contribution.

We see this operating within the life of the church, the family and the workplace. Some people seem to have the gift of vision. They dream dreams and see what is possible and what needs to be done. Others are leaders. They are able to mobilize and galvanize people into practical action. Some are great administrators while others are carers or healers. The list of possibilities is almost limitless. But the point is clear. It is very unusual for a visionary to be a leader, administrator and carer all rolled into one.

It is far more evident that we have certain gifts, talents and abilities but seem to lack others. This should not be a problem for it allows us to work in cooperation with others. But it can be difficult if one has an ego problem, or if one is placed in the unenviable position of having to do every-thing because others are not able or willing to contribute.

We can so easily keep church members from exercising their gifts by not giving them power or responsibility. We may also cling to particular roles and tasks within the family and not allow the other partner to participate and contribute.

The challenge for us, therefore, is to make sure that we do not try to be and do everything. We should not dominate nor dictate but should instead encourage others to make their contribution.

Prayer: Lord, help me in the exercise of my gifts and responsibilities to realize that I play only a small part in the overall scheme of things. Help me to be faithful without excluding others in what you've called me. AMEN.

REFLECTION 90

STRAIGHT PATHS FOR OUR FEET:

Accepting God's discipline and grace

"Make level paths for your feet," so that the lame may not be disabled, but rather healed.

Hebrews 12:13

The Christian life is one of joy and responsibility. On the one hand, we freely receive God's grace, encouragement and benediction. But on the other hand, we learn through experience the meaning of responsibility, hard work, commitment, and the need to persevere. Some Christians seek God's blessing without personal responsibility, while others try to live responsibly without God's grace. Clearly these two elements belong together in the journey of life.

But we do sometimes run the race of life with unnecessary handicaps or traverse over especially difficult terrain. The writer to the Hebrews suggests that we need to throw off needless burdens (Hebrews 12:1) and make the paths level especially for the lame among us. He gives us other helpful guidelines.

He points out the importance of our response to God's discipline. We need to learn from God's dealings in our lives and to lay things aside, otherwise we have to go over the same ground again and again. Moreover we must cultivate a life free from impurity (12:

14). This has to do with maintaining and developing godly values not only in our thought life and our relationships but also in our work or business. A life without holiness and moral integrity will only burden us down. It will also sidetrack us. And sadly it will repay us doubly in disappointment.

The writer, furthermore, challenges us to live free from bitterness (12:15). This aids our progress in the present and makes us open to the future. Bitterness only binds us to the past with its hurts and disappointments. Not only does it destroy relationships, it also poisons the well of our own being.

Finally, a level path is secured when we take to our hearts whatever blessing God has given us. We dare not reject the grace of God (12:16-17). What this means is that we learn to embrace thankfully what God has given us in the form of talents, gifts, life experiences and calling, and not to look with envy at what others have.

To follow these strategies is to help make a straight path for our feet. This is not to suggest that our life will be easy, but we will make it less hard for ourselves. For wisdom, integrity, hope and the glad acceptance of God's blessing make for a lightness of step even if the journey is tougher than we had first thought.

Prayer: Lord, in the journey of life, help us not to make things harder, but rather avail ourselves of your grace. AMEN.

REFLECTION 91

SENSITIVITY:

Being careful in what we say

Do not pay attention to every word people say, or you may hear your servant cursing you for you know in your heart that many times you yourself have cursed others.

Ecclesiastes 7:21-22

Words are not without their power. They can bring healing and encouragement. They also can bring destruction. They can tear down, humiliate and bring confusion; they can also bring hope, peace and direction. We therefore need to be careful with our words.

Everywhere in the New Testament we are reminded that Christ's work in our lives should affect the way we speak to one another. "But now you must rid yourselves of all such things as these: anger, rage, malice, slander, and filthy language from your lips. Do not lie to each other, since you have taken off your old self with its practices" (Colossians 3:8-9). Our speaking should be characterized by encouragement, love, truth and challenge. James injects a note of sober realism and reminds us that we often do not have our speaking under control (James 3:2)—this especially so when we are at home or among friends. There we are more open and less careful in what we say. There we have more room for repartee, punning, retort, irony, wit and jest. There too we give more pointed and honest responses.

All of this can be quite appropriate, but needs to be governed by a loving sensitivity which we develop as we relate to one another. Sensitivity plays such a critical role in determining what can be said or left unsaid. This needs practical wisdom and spiritual empathy.

Prayer: Lord, in the whole way I relate to others, including my speaking, make me more honest and sensitive. AMEN.

REFLECTION 92

OVERCOMING OUR FEARS:
Living a purposeful life

And even the very hairs of your head are all numbered. So don't be afraid; you are worth more than many sparrows.
                                                     Matthew 10:30-31

Of all the things that motivate us—needs, fears, interests and a sense of calling—fear is probably the most negative. This is not to suggest that every fear is destructive. A healthy fear of danger can be protective; certain fears can stimulate us to greater effort. But there are fears which are crippling and debilitating.

Some fears were instilled in us when we were young. Others we have acquired along the way. Some fears are totally vague; others, specific and recurring. Sadly, fears can be self-fulfilling. Jesus addresses the matter of fear in situations that are themselves fear-inspiring. He speaks of rejection, betrayal and persecution, and instructs us that when confronted with such occasions, we need not be afraid (Matthew 10:16-25).

His reasons for suggesting that we need not be afraid are even more surprising. First, He reminds us that the power of fear will be weakened when things are exposed and come into the light (10:26). He is certainly right. Fears are fed by misinformation, mystery and lack of understanding. When through insight and discernment, the bases of our fears are laid bare, we are on the path towards overcoming them. Secondly, Jesus suggests that if we have lost our life in true discipleship, we cannot lose it again. There is then nothing more to fear (10:28). Finally, he tells us that fear is cast out by being secure in the Father's love for us (10:29-31).

If we can overcome our fears and have our needs met as we pursue a calling which is characterized by other-person centredness rather than self-interest, there is no reason why our lives should not be purposeful and fruitful.

***Prayer:** Lord, grant that my life may not be controlled by fear but by your purpose and calling. AMEN.*

REFLECTION 93

FINDING JESUS:

When we truly seek him

He appointed twelve—designating them apostles—that they might be with him.

Mark 3:14a

We should desire to be with Jesus. But where in the world is he? Where do we find him? Clearly he is not at our beck and call. We can not just open the Bible and find him there. He does not always appear in church. He does not always come through in the preaching and is not always present in our praying. Jesus is never automatically there where we expect to find him.

But he is there where sometimes we least expect to meet him. Clearly he is there where people seek him rather than expect him. He seems to come to those who, in their brokenness and despair, feel they have no claim on him. The poor, the needy, the widow and the fatherless seem to have an uncanny ability of meeting him, while those of us who have been in the church for years and know our Bible backward and forward, seem to be hard-pressed to meet up with him. However, this often does not seem to bother us too much, for our comfortable lives go on regardless. This is probably our biggest obstacle. For so often Jesus is convenient but not vitally necessary. We would like him around to comfort and to bless us, but we can run our lives quite well without his words and direction.

Jesus is, therefore, elusive to us. But he readily meets with those who simply can not and do not want to live without him. When Jesus is invited to come in from the periphery of our lives, we will find him to be already centrally present.

Prayer: Lord, teach me how to live so that you are the core of my being and my concerns. AMEN.

REFLECTION 94

ALL SCRIPTURE:

Responding to a kaleidoscope of wisdom

All Scripture is God-breathed and is useful for teaching, rebuking, correcting and training in righteous- ness, so that the man of God may be thoroughly equipped for every good work.

2 Timothy 3:16-17

Scripture talks to us about life's big issues: life's meaning and purpose, suffering, death, reconciliation, attitudes toward possessions and the right use of power and influence. Central to life's meaning is God's loving involvement in our lives and in our world. Scripture is God's divine recipe for living. It is not simply a book about the future life. It sets before us how God acted in the past and how his people responded. It challenges us to embrace God's vision for our lives and encourages us to express that in faithfulness and integrity.

The Bible is not a quick fix-it book for our ills and troubles. It is more a handbook on life showing us how to live. It gives us the practical wisdom of Proverbs; the heartcry of the Psalmist; the sober lessons of Israel's history; the centrality of freedom in Christ in the Epistles; care for the poor in Luke; the power of the Holy Spirit in Acts; the practical Christianity of James; the call to love God and others in John; and the power of faith in Hebrews.

Scripture presents us with a vision of life that recognizes God's presence and purpose in all of it. It speaks to us about the importance of faith in Christ, the empowerment of the Holy Spirit, the significance of prayer, the quality of our lifestyle, our task in society, concern for justice, care for God's world, sharing the Good News, our roles in our families, the proper attitude toward the state, and hospitality as our ministry.

From this wealth of wisdom we can draw direction for our lives. Let us therefore join the psalmist and declare, "I meditate on your precepts and consider your ways. I delight in your decrees; I will not neglect your word" (119:15-16).

Prayer: Lord, give me a hunger for your Word and ways. AMEN.

PASSION

REFLECTION 95

THERE'S MORE TO LOVE:
Be bold and passionate

Love is patient, love is kind. It does not envy, it does not boast, it is not proud. It is not rude, it is not self-seeking, it is not easily angered, it keeps no record of wrongs.

1 Corinthians 13:4-5

Love is an oft-repeated word, but an elusive reality in our times. It can mean almost anything from a quick sexual encounter to total self- sacrifice.

Scripture's emphasis is on love as a self-giving regard for the other. This is expressed in 1 Corinthians 13, the Bible's love chapter. Here Paul describes love by the qualities of patience and kindness. He notes that such love is not envious, boastful, proud, rude, self-seeking or easily angered. It does not rejoice in wrong but is protective, trusting, hopeful and persevering.

Yet, this is hardly an adequate description of love. Not only is love described here in mainly negative terms (what it does *not* do), it is the love of restraint. It is love as an exercise of self- control. It is love showing carefulness and sensitivity. And it is the exercise of power over our selves for the sake and well-being of the other.

The reason for this emphasis lies in the context of 1 Corinthians 13 where Paul attempts to place restraint on the spiritual enthusiasm of the Corinthians (see Chapters 12 and 14).

But love has other facets. There is also commitment and passion. Some situations require love to be bold rather than patient; passionate, rather than kind; affirming, rather than withholding; challenging, rather than sensitive; brave, rather than gentle; generous and spontaneous, rather than careful.

This facet of love will do radical things (1 Corinthians 13:3). It will, for example, give everything it has to the poor or make commitments of total self-sacrifice. Such love is not restrained but passionate. Clearly, both facets are vital. For carefulness without boldness will never accomplish much, and boldness without carefulness may be destructive.

Prayer: Lord, make me sensitive and bold. AMEN.

REFLECTION 96

ZEAL FOR YOUR HOUSE:

Be bold in God's service

His disciples remembered that it is written: "Zeal for your house will consume me."

John 2:17

Being a Christian has little to do with being "nice." This is particularly so when being "nice" means colourless, lacking in conviction and merely socially acceptable. Being a Christian has more to do with conviction, passion and zeal than with anything else.

Yet this is precisely what our age finds so unacceptable. For it fears fanaticism and intolerance. But zeal and intolerance need not be the same. In fact, they are quite different. Intolerance usually implies that one holds immovably to some narrow perception of life, while zeal connotes high motivation regarding universal concerns.

Jesus was zealous. He was jealously concerned about the honour of God. He had a passion for righteousness. He was deeply concerned about love, mercy and justice. He was characterized by the conviction that the world order needed to be transformed to become God's kingdom of peace and righteousness. His concerns were wide enough to embrace all, even those who were socially outcast. Yet, Jesus could hardly be called intolerant. That is a description more fitting for Jesus' enemies, the Pharisees. Their narrowness of vision and self-righteousness made them insensitive to the genuine concerns of others. Their intolerance excluded all who could not, or would not, embrace their legalistic vision of life.

The challenge then that faces us is not to become so afraid of being people of zeal and conviction that we become anemic and "nice." At the same time, we need to avoid becoming overly concerned about peripheral issues. The Pharisees had the ability to major on minors. We should be zealous about the big issues such as those that mobilized Jesus into action. To be passionate about God's universal concern for love, mercy and justice may not win us a popularity contest, but may gain us some grudging admiration from those who do not hold our religious convictions.

Prayer: Lord, so often I am motivated by what other people may think of me. Help me to embrace your concerns for the world and not be afraid. Help me to do what I need to do to honour your name and entrust the consequences to you. AMEN.

REFLECTION 97

A SIGNIFICANT MINORITY

Learning to be out of step

I will surely bring together the remnant of Israel.

Micah 2:12b

There is little point in being different for its own sake. That may only display our insecurity or stubbornness. But to be committed to a dull uniformity can be equally unfortunate. Moreover, the majority is not always right.

In Israel's history, God often dealt with only a remnant of his people. Throughout the history of the Christian church, it is significant minorities that often distinctly demonstrated God's light and truth. There are always some people who can see issues a little more clearly and have better insight into how the church can be faithful.

The point is that we need to become men and women of vision, conviction and integrity. The church is not best served, nor God's cause adequately promoted by simply going along with whatever everyone else is doing. This means that we need to rediscover the cutting edge of our faith. We must reread the Bible critically. We must also rediscover the impulses that transformed the church in the past. Moreover, we need to develop the courage to stand for our convictions. Such convictions should not remain at the level of rhetoric but be translated into action.

This is not to suggest that any and every radical idea and personal oddity is to be championed. It is rather a matter of realizing that the present Christian tradition may need change or enrichment. The present emphasis on Christian prosperity, for example, would be dramatically changed if we read the early church fathers' critique on riches and property especially when these were accumulated by exploiting others.

In developing a clear perspective on God's will for our times we need to listen to Scripture and use the wisdom of the past. In forging our stance, we should not be afraid to be out of step with present directions and emphases. The present church can never be automatically right. It will only be right if it lives obediently to God's Word and resists the spirit of this age.

Prayer: Lord, help me to become a person of integrity and conviction. Help me to live my convictions with grace and humility. AMEN.

REFLECTION 98

THE HEROES:

Inspired by the lives of others

Therefore, since we are surrounded by such a great cloud of witnesses
Hebrews 12:1

Every generation needs its heroes, its outstanding men and women to whom it can look for inspiration and hope. Christians are no exception. Throughout the history of the church they have looked back to the normative example of Jesus Christ and his apostles. But they have also drawn inspiration and hope from its past and contemporary sons and daughters: Augustine, Luther, Wesley, Hudson Taylor, Dietrich Bonhoeffer, Martin Luther King, Mother Teresa.

We must not regard these outstanding people as larger than life. But to fail to be inspired by the life and example of Christians who have left their mark not only on the church but also on the world can simply be a reflection of our own narrow pettiness and mediocrity.

Carlyle once noted that "no sadder proof can be given by a man of his own littleness than disbelief in great men." Women are not exempt from this. In the church we certainly need our heroes for they demonstrate to us the realm of the possible. They embody for us an outstanding response to the call of Christ. They have shown in their lifetime a response to the needs of their world in the light of the Gospel of Christ.

By reading about them, we re-enter their world, their faith, their struggles and their victories, and we cannot but be inspired to live the life of faith in our own time. While we can only be truly empowered by Christ himself, we can certainly have our faith enriched by his followers to lift our vision higher.

Prayer: Lord, thank you for the many faithful women and men who have served you in every age. Help me to live for you to my fullest capacity. AMEN.

REFLECTION 99

CHRISTIAN, TAKE YOUR STAND:
Being passionate about God's kingdom

Therefore put on the full armor of God, so that when the day of evil comes, you may be able to stand your ground, and after you have done everything, to stand.

Ephesians 6:13

Christians are not only to take a stand *for* some things, they are also to take a stand *against* certain things. We are for righteousness, justice and peace, and against unrighteousness, exploitation and oppression. What we are to be against, however, is sometimes difficult to discern for unrighteousness has a chameleon quality. It changes in different times and cultures.

Luther was right when he said that every age has its particular sins and evils that need to be resisted. In contemporary American culture that might be the need to resist the pressure to succeed and be popular. In Australia that might take the form of overcoming our lazy attitude towards life. In the Philippines that might mean being willing to stand against the values of the group.

Let me identify some broad issues in which we need to take a stand. We need to elevate grace over law since most of us are legalists at heart. We need to strive for the greater vision of love, justice and mercy above our penchant for systems and routines (Matthew 23:23). We also need to promote participation over selfish individualism. The idea that I am complete and need no one else violates the very nature of the Trinity. It negates God's participation with us and the reality that the Body of Christ is a community of believers (1 Corinthians 12:13).

We, moreover, need to prioritize action over intention. Desire is no substitute for doing. That our inner attitudes are right does not take away the necessity for practical action. Jesus ends his Sermon on the Mount with a commendation for the person who *did* what was commanded (Matthew 7:24,28). We also need to celebrate involvement over against asceticism. Withdrawal from life in order to be holy is merely saving ourselves. Rather, we should abandon ourselves to God and throw ourselves into meeting the needs and challenges of our age (1 Corinthians 5:9-10).

Furthermore, we need to encourage all believers to exercise their priesthood instead of promoting the idea of having spiritual specialists. We should not divide the church into doers and onlookers, saints and sinners, or clergy and laity. While the New Testament does make distinctions between the weak and the strong, babes in Christ and mature Christians, it encourages the participation of all believers.

Finally, we need to reject every form of procrastination and determinism. We cannot argue that it doesn't matter what we do because God will work things out. Nor should we put our lives on hold because we believe that Jesus is coming back. We need to take our stand *for* grace, participation, meaningful action, equality and responsibility.

Prayer: Lord, help me to resist the spirit and values of this age; help me to stand for the values of your kingdom. AMEN.

REFLECTION 100

RESTORATION IS ALSO FOR THE OTHER:

Commitment to service

He who has been stealing must steal no longer, but must work, doing something useful with his own hands, that he may have something to share with those in need.

Ephesians 4:28

There are some endeavours which are out of bounds for the Christian. Stealing, in its many sophisticated or its rather naive methods, is one. Such activity must be replaced with useful work.

This change, however, is not simply for the well-being of the person concerned. It is also for the other. Thieves, alcoholics, drug addicts, criminals, and those who commit the more socially-accepted sins of tax evasion, lying, envy, hypocrisy and self-righteousness are called to repent and change. This, however, is not so that they can then live self-sufficient lives. Thieves are not to be converted so they can then become comfortable and selfish.

Our task in our work with the needy, disadvantaged and social deviants is not to turn people into conservative middle-class Christians. Repentance from sin and evil social practices and attitudes is meant to free people for radically new possibilities of living. Reformation from the risky "business" of theft as vocation is meant to plunge them into the equally risky adventure of living by faith marked by generosity and sharing.

The conversion of a thief is not to make that person a penny-pinching accountant. Conversion is not swapping one bondage for another. It should rather free us to live life with a whole new set of values. This includes concern for the other. The ex-thief is exhorted to work, not so much to become rich, as to share with others in need. True conversion will always be characterized, not by the well-being of the one converted, but by his or her service to others.

Prayer: Lord, may the changes in my life lead not just to a relief from my problems, but to lifestyle changes that truly serve others. AMEN.

REFLECTION 101

IN THE PRESENT:

Being thankful for God's daily provision

Give us today our daily bread. Forgive us our debts, as we also have forgiven our debtors.

Matthew 6:11-12

We should live with boldness towards the future and with thankfulness regarding the past.

We also need to come to terms with the present. We should not trivialize the present by looking wistfully back to past times which seem to us better or more exciting. Nor should we dream of immediate answers, better circumstances and easy solutions regarding the future. Instead, we should discover God's grace and purpose for this day and this age, not only for tomorrow and the age to come.

We are encouraged to seek and be thankful for God's provisions for this day (Matthew 6:11). We are called to the responsibilities of this day (Luke 12:47-48). Each new day not only brings its unique opportunities for us to do what we should, but also promises God's participation and care (2 Corinthians 6:2).

There are also some things that need to be limited to this day, namely, its failures and sins. While the positive things of each day will prepare us for a better future, the negatives of each day need to be nipped in the bud. Each day has its evil (Matthew 6:34); we are encouraged to settle this with God and those we have wronged today (Ephesians 4:26).

Grateful for the past and hopeful for the future, we can thank God for what we could accomplish today. And we can be glad that the failures of this day can be forgiven.

Prayer: Lord, this is the day that you have made. Help me to undo the bad and to preserve the good of this day. AMEN.

ACTION

REFLECTION 102

THOUGH FAR FROM PERFECT:

Acting in a fallen world

In the place of judgment—wickedness was there, in the place of justice—wickedness was there.
Ecclesiastes 3:16

We long for a perfect world where good triumphs and where evil is eradicated. But such a world is not yet—not even in the church or in our own hearts. Even where the name of God is praised, his life celebrated, his word heard and his name honoured, we experience imperfection. In the secret recesses of our own hearts and in our daily living, we know that sin is yet with us. Thus we should hardly be surprised that justice languishes and is not always instituted in our land.

But the all-pervasive reality of evil should not commit us to passivity. The presence of the imperfect should not commit us to resignation. Change is possible even though its culmination awaits the fullness of time (Romans 8:18-25).

As Christians we sometimes think that we have little right to say anything to others because not everything is in order in our own lives. However, the church will never be a perfect institution on earth, and we will never bear the marks of final perfection in this life. Yet, act and speak we must!

If God is concerned about justice, then we must also be, even though in the cause of social or economic justice, we may not be wholly free from the reality of prejudice and unfair dealing. If God is for the poor, then so must we be, even though we make it into a cause that lacks appropriate human compassion. If God is for purity, then so must we be pure, in all its social and personal ramifications, even when impurity still lurks within our own heart. If God is for joyful generosity, then we need to be generous, even though we give grudgingly and are plagued with second thoughts about being gullible.

We need to continue to act in our world even when we are far from perfect. This should make all of our activities characterized by humility and open to change and adjustment. Our plans for change may never be fully right, but act we must!

Prayer: Lord, we do want to see good prevail in our world even as we long for perfection. AMEN.

REFLECTION 103

A CRITICAL PERSPECTIVE ON OUR CULTURE:

Living by God's values

But we have the mind of Christ.

1 Corinthians 2:16b

We all have our beginnings in a certain family, tradition and culture. Many of us come from normal suburban homes, and have typical middle class values. Yet most of us never reflect on whether these values are appropriate, or whether they are in line with the ethics of the New Testament. We simply take our worldview for granted. "The way things are is the way they are meant to be."

But we should never take our cultural values for granted. They need to be questioned. There is every good reason to ask whether our values of independence and self-sufficiency are good.

In this questioning process, we would do well to listen to our secular as well as our spiritual prophets. Theodore Roszak, in *Where the Wasteland Ends*, stirs secular society against a materialism that devalues life's purpose and meaning: "When the transcendent energies waste away, then too the person shrivels—though far less obviously. Their loss is suffered in privacy and bewildered silence; it is easily submerged in affluence, entertaining diversions, and adjustive therapy."

William Holmes, in *Tomorrow's Church,* suggests that our suburban way of life can be very narrow. He writes, "One of the sicknesses of suburbia is its preoccupation with narrow gauge emotional needs which preclude the larger realities." He continues that "suburbia has a cultic inwardness and self-preoccupation," and further that suburbia is a "residential island providing a haven that cuts us off from conceptual risks."

One only needs to work in a different culture, or with the poor to gain a much more critical perspective on our normal values. A more careful reading of the Bible should also challenge us to evaluate what we so easily take for granted. The point, however, is that as Christians who have been renewed by Christ and who have received his life-giving Spirit, we need to have our values changed to conform with God's values. We, therefore, dare not simply assume that our suburban values harmonize with God's. It is more likely that they don't. Thus we need to evaluate, probe, question, wrestle with Scripture and have our minds renewed and horizons expanded so that we can embrace God's larger vision of life and begin to act accordingly.

Prayer: Lord, help me to overcome my narrow concerns, and grant me a vision of your concern for the world. AMEN.

REFLECTION 104

OPPORTUNISM:

Doing things in our strength

All you who light fires and . . . walk in the light of your fires . . . will lie down in torment.

Isaiah 50:11

We can easily take over when God appears to be silent. This is a temptation for all who are involved in any form of Christian service. We make things happen in our own strength. Soul power can become a substitute for the Spirit's power, and we can prophesy on our own when God has nothing to say. We can perform miracles without God (Matthew 7:21,23).

This kind of opportunism is usually motivated by the desire to continue to appear successful in the service of God. It is a temptation we need to resist. Isaiah shows us the only way we can go. "Let him who walks in the dark," he tells us, "who has no light, trust in the name of the LORD and rely on his God" (50:10b). But he continues, don't go creating your own light and seek to walk in it. This will only lead to destruction (50:11).

If God is silent then we should be quiet as well. If there is no light, no word, no healing, no answer and no power, then we can only trust in the Lord and wait patiently for him. We can not pretend that everything is as usual. We certainly should not make things happen in the name of God when God is not at work.

Whatever we may do can never be a substitute for God's action and blessing. In fact, we will labour in vain if the Lord does not build the house (Psalm 127:1). Our attempts to drum up what people expect will not give life to them and will become destructive for us. A true servant of God can only give that which he or she has first received.

Prayer: Lord, grant that I may not try to step into your shoes and make things happen apart from your will and action. AMEN.

REFLECTION 105

INCARNATION:

A practical strategy for transformation

The word became flesh and lived for a while among us.
John 1:14a

Clarence Jordan, who in the 1960s championed black rights in racist Georgia, U.S.A., once made the simple but profound observation that God never sent a letter to communicate good news. He sent a person. God's strategy was not words but concrete action. The Incarnation was God's method of mission.

Jesus demonstrated the love and concern of his Father by dwelling among the people of his day. In fulfilling our mission, we can do no less.

I remember consulting with a group of enthusiastic young volunteers who every Saturday night conducted a drop-in centre in what had become almost a ghost town some forty kilo-meters away. Having nothing to do, with no entertainment and sports facilities, many of the town's young people crowded the drop-in centre. Many came from broken homes. Some were already alcoholics. The youth workers indicated that they wanted to do something more for them, but my suggestion came as a shock. I suggested that some should go and live in the town so that long-term contacts could be made and long-term helping strategies implemented.

I explained that this was the kind of strategy that Jesus adopted. He didn't occasionally speak to the poor but became poor himself, and so was close enough to bring them new life.

It is in living with people and thus entering their everyday world that we can, together with them, work for change. While we should never belittle the value of practical aid which is given to the destitute, this rates a poor second to the strategy of incarnational mission.

To live in hope and faith with the needy, to enter their world, to share their fears and aspirations and to prayerfully and practically work for personal and societal change is to walk in the footsteps of the Man who stilled the waters, made the blind to see and the deaf to hear, and who brought Good News to the poor.

Prayer: Lord, teach me not just to give things to others but to give myself as well. AMEN.

REFLECTION 106

A SNAKE IN EVERY PARADISE:

Serving in the face of opposition

Do not allow what you consider good to be spoken of as evil.
                                                    Romans 14:16

The human condition is a strange mixture of good and evil, hope and despair, beauty and tragedy. The human story, as it is told in the Bible, underscores this fact.

Paradise was marked by disobedience. Abraham's life of faith was traumatized by Lot's greed. The joy of Israel's deliverance from Egypt was shattered by their murmuring and disobedience in the wilderness. The vision of the new nation as a kingdom of priests was ruined by the desire for an earthly king. Faithfulness to God's law was marred by religious idolatry.

David, the psalmist was also David, the adulterer. The vision of social justice and righteousness of the prophets was undermined by the intransigence of a powerful elite. The popularity of Jesus turned into scorn and rejection. The sharing community of the early church became the sacramental institution some centuries later. What all this means is that in spite of the presence of good, evil lies so close at hand.

Our own personal history is hardly different. Our strengths usually mask some very real weaknesses. Our best actions can also have unfortunate and unintended consequences. Our visions and dreams never quite materialize in the way we expected. There is a snake in every paradise.

This need not drive us to despair, but it should guard us against building our Utopias. It allows us to hope for much, but not for perfection. It allows us to do what is good, while we confess our wrong motivations. This should make us more careful and discerning. Pascal issues some relevant warnings. He notes, "When we try to push virtues to extremes in either direction, vices appear." He further points out that the most difficult form of evil to discover is "what is known as good."

Nietzsche, moreover, reminds us that "extreme positions are not succeeded by moderate ones but by extreme positions of the opposite kind." Thus morality can become despotism. Spirituality can become "pharisaism." Good deeds can become oppressive. Spiritual self-renunciation can become self-rejection.

In our quest to please God and serve humanity, we need to be discerning not only regarding what we do, but how we do it. We need to be careful not only in how we do it, but also in what may be the anticipated results. Even then we may need to pray that God may save us from our own results.

Prayer: Lord, I acknowledge that good does not follow even from my good actions unless your grace is present. Please transform the work of my hands into that which is lasting, beautiful and good. AMEN.

REFLECTION 107

MORE THAN CIRCUMSTANCES:
When God accompanies us

"Here comes that dreamer!" they said to each other. "Come now, let's kill him and throw him into one of these cisterns and say that a ferocious animal devoured him. Then we'll see what comes of his dreams.

Genesis 37:19-20

Joseph's life despite its privileged background did not get off to a good start. He was spoiled by his father. He was jealously hated by his brothers. A son of a well-to-do *haciendero*, he was deported from his own country and was reduced to slavery. His good efforts in Potiphar's household came to ruin through sexual intrigue and were rewarded by imprisonment. And his helpful efforts in assisting the wine steward were repaid with being conveniently forgotten for another two years while he eked out an existence in the king's maximum security prison.

One might well expect that with such misfortune, Joseph's life would end in bitterness, despair and disaster. But this was not the case. Joseph's life was more than its circumstances. He had an inner strength. Joseph was a young man who heard from God and thus was sustained by him. In spite of his circumstances, he remained buoyant and positive. God's blessing was with him in such evident ways that Potiphar (Genesis 39:3-4), the jailer (Genesis 39:20b-

21) and the king (Genesis 41:38-40) could not fail to recognize it. Joseph brought material blessing to Potiphar's household, moral hope to a prison, reconciliation to his family, material well-being to Egypt, and salvation for the Israelites from the scourge of hunger.

Joseph prefigures the way that we as Christians can act in our world. We, too, need to hear God's voice for our time, overcome despair in difficult circumstances, creatively respond to suffering, celebrate God's presence with us in ways that bring blessing to others, make an impact for good in our work or career and in the social institutions of our land, and seek to affect the political destiny of our nation. In the life of Joseph are powerful lessons, in particular, that difficulty need not be permanent. Hope in God's promises can sustain us to the point of victory.

Prayer: Lord, grant that my circumstances may not determine what is possible, but rather may your Word and promises sustain me. AMEN.

REFLECTION 108

GOD'S PATTERN

The shaping of our lives

To this you were called, because Christ suffered for you, leaving you an example, that you should follow in his steps.

1 Peter 2:21

Nature manifests a discernible pattern. Spring precedes summer, and winter follows fall, just as growth follows germination, and fruit-bearing completes the cycle.

While the social world is more complex than the seasons of nature, God's involvement in our spiritual development is not without its pattern and design. After all, our life is to be patterned after Christ. Paul called Christians to imitate him as he sought to imitate his Master.

There are some discernible steps in the way God wishes to shape our lives. First, he calls us to become a participant in his way of life. This means that we have to recognize the bankruptcy of our own ways, the futility of our self-righteousness, the hollowness of our fun and frivolity, and the reality of our guilt. We need to turn and embrace Christ's death, participate in his friendship, sit at his table and be drenched by his Spirit.

Secondly, we need to learn God's ways. This requires a deep attachment to the Teacher, relinquishing personal goals and ambitions, and getting involved in furthering the Master's cause.

As participants we cannot simply be there for the ride, for our relationship to Jesus binds us to his purposes and concerns.

Thirdly, God's pattern for us is to be reproducers. What we have learned, we need to pass on. After being trained, we can train others. Having been shaped by God's discipline, we can influence others. Having received, we are called to give. Having suffered and endured, we can comfort others.

Christian growth and development is not haphazard. As he deals with us in our particular personality needs and idiosyncrasies, God seeks to bring us from immaturity to wholeness, and from being mere recipients to joyful givers.

Prayer: Lord, thank you that you care about me personally. I also thank you for working in me in a way that is consistent with the way you work in other people's lives. AMEN.

REFLECTION 109

TRANSFORMATION:

Building a new world

The nations will walk by its light, and the kings of the earth will bring their splendour into it.

Revelation 21:24

The Bible is utterly realistic. A new world is not fully possible apart from God's final intervention when new heavens and a new earth will come into being.

This does not mean that we do nothing now to better the world. And we certainly should not stand idly by while things get worse. There is no virtue in passivity. Instead, we are called to transform the world even though we know that this task can never be fully accomplished by us.

The place to start with change is first of all for us to be changed. We need to be renewed and for-given, and to be empowered by the Holy Spirit. We need to gain a whole new vision of life in the light of the kingdom of God.

But changed individuals won't necessarily change the world unless they deal with their selfishness and become outward-looking. A new person in Christ who embraces a "bless-me" kind of spirituality and belongs to a world-denying church has little social impact.

The new life in Christ should empower us for a life of obedience and service where we seek to make an impact on our families, our neighbourhoods and our wider community. In embracing a world-affirming Christianity, we recognize that it is our task to see that godly values permeate our places of work and the institutions of our land.

Thus we need to be proactive but non-conformist. We need to see new possibilities that come from reflecting on Scripture and from living a life of faith and prayer.

When God is working with us, barriers can be removed and change is possible, but only if the change sought for is in accordance with God's will.

Prayer: *Thank you, Lord, for opportunities to serve you in our troubled world. Make me your instrument in my family, neighbourhood and place of work. Help me to be bold and unafraid in working for your kingdom to come among us.*

AMEN

REFLECTION 110

EMPOWERMENT:

Seeking the Spirit's power

I am going to send you what my Father has promised; but stay in the city until you have been clothed with power from on high.
                                            Luke 24:49

In this book of reflections, I have emphasized the importance of the roles that we are to play in the world and how we are to live responsibly. This is not to suggest, however, that we are to be self-sufficient and certainly not self-willed in the exercise of our responsibilities.

To be responsible means to be treated by God as adults and not as immature children. It also means that God has entrusted tasks to us. He has placed in our hands the responsibility to share the Good News of Jesus Christ. We also have the responsibility to shape the church and to transform the world.

But these things we can not do by ourselves. We are therefore called to a life of faith and prayer seeking to discern God's will and to receive the Holy Spirit's empowerment.

There is nothing more significant than to do God's will. And there is nothing more powerful than to do what God asks of us in his strength.

This means that we need the Spirit's power. The Spirit is the One whom Christ will pour out upon us when we have come to the end of our own resources. The Spirit will be there when our self-sufficiency has crumbled and when, in prayer, we acknowledge that we can not accomplish what we ought apart from God's participation.

While we may act into life in a variety of ways, our most powerful activity will be that which is done in the power of the Spirit. Therefore, part of our responsibility is to seek God's enabling in all that we do.

Prayer: Holy Spirit, breathe upon me and guide and empower me in all that you want me to do. AMEN.